Southern Living®
Cookbook
Library

The
Deep South
Cookbook

Cover: Banquet Broilers (page 122)

contents

preface

What is the Deep South? For many people, the term refers to a vast geographical region. But for the people of the Deep South, it is a shared culture, a common heritage of history and traditions. And it is the culinary aspect of this legacy that is explored in *The Deep South Cookbook.*

Here are generations-old recipes, many of them have rarely appeared in print before. They have been assembled so that homemakers everywhere can enjoy the region's rich culinary treasures. Accompanying the recipes are pages that describe how the region was settled and developed. Begin your tour through the Deep South by reading about the Englishmen who colonized Maryland, Virginia, and the Carolinas and relive with them the wonders they found there: seafood, game birds, animals, and other foods. All this plenty inevitably found its way to colonial dinner tables and eventually to a cuisine of the Deep South. Read on and you can move through the mountains and valleys with the brave men and women who settled western Virginia, Tennessee, and Kentucky. See how the recipes they carried with them were adapted to the new foods they found.

For everyone who lives in this region and for all those who have ever marveled at it, this is a cookbook to cherish. From our kitchens to yours, welcome to the wonderful world of cooking – Deep South style.

Unlike many American regions, the South is not a small pocket of settlements that grew together to form an industrialized section nor is it a physically isolated area. Southerners will tell you that the South is a state of mind, a shared attitude toward life and the things of which life consists. Yet it is possible to find that in certain states, this attitude is more prevalent than in others: it is these states, indicated on the accompanying map that we have designated as the Deep South.

Here tables are aptly termed "groaning boards." They are filled with foods of diverse origins — infinite varieties of breads, vegetables, meat, fish — all served in sufficient quantity to ensure that not even the last-minute guest goes hungry.

the deep south

THE ORIGINS OF A TRADITION

The evolution of southern hospitality probably has its roots in the nature of the region itself. For all its charming yet up-to-date cities, the Deep South is essentially rural. The earliest settlers here, the Englishmen who populated the coastal tidewater regions, built plantations under an elaborate system of land grants to ensure that the rural nature of these areas would be preserved. As a result homes were few and many miles of wilderness separated one from the other. When people are remote from each other, hospitality comes naturally.

As adventurous settlers pushed out of the tidewater settlements into the Appalachians and down into Spanish-dominated Florida, the tradition of hospitality went with them. Even in remote frontier settlements in this area along the fringes of the Indian nations, the family's meal was eagerly shared with the traveler — who was in turn asked to share his news of happenings throughout the colonies.

Attracted by reports of rich soil and plentiful land grants in the Deep South, emigrants flocked here from many European nations. Strangers in a strange land, these newcomers one and all received a warm welcome from hospitable Southerners. Soon it mattered little whether a wanderer found himself in the staunchly English settlements of the tidewater or in the distinctively German community of Ebenezer on the Savannah River — he would be welcome and made to feel at home.

THE SOUTHERN FOODS

Perhaps the warm welcome of southern people reflected, in part, nature's hospitality to them. Here the climate was gentle with enough sunshine, rainfall, and warmth to produce not just one good crop a year but two or even three. Natural abundance also made the South a veritable storehouse of foods. From the sparkling rivers came catfish, bream, perch, black bass, and trout. Tidewater flats and offshore beds yielded oysters, shrimp, crabs, and crayfish. From the game-rich woodlands and marshes came deer, wild ducks, geese, partridges, doves, and wild turkey. These ever-present foods were combined with the crops raised in almost every community to give southern tables an aura of natural plenty.

Corn was the most prominent of the foods found throughout southern cooking. So, too, were green vegetables. But each section of the Deep South, depending on its history, traditions, and the customs of the people who settled there, developed its individual ways of preparing foods.

favorite foods
of maryland

The foods of Maryland reflect both the traditions of the people who settled the area and their use of native foods. Maryland families take enormous pride in their recipes, many of which have passed down through the generations. Each generation adds its own touches to these recipes, updating them or introducing new ingredients. The result is often a recipe that combines the best of modern and old-fashioned cooking.

The choicest of these recipes, shared by homemakers from throughout the Deep South, is yours in this section. Many of the recipes come from Marylanders who still live on the land their families settled hundreds of years ago. Others come from women whose families left Maryland for other parts of the Deep South. But all are home-tested, family-approved, and the pride of the homemakers who have signed them.

As you browse through the pages, the types of dishes you'll find recalls the plentitude that greeted early settlers in Maryland. As would be expected, seafood plays a prominent role in the cookery, and is featured here in such dishes as Savory Turtle Soup, Fried Soft-shell Crabs, and Maryland Crab Cakes.

These and other recipes will take you on a "cook's tour" of Maryland, an unforgettable trip to the first of the Deep South's distinctive cookeries.

Maryland must have seemed an Eden to the Englishmen who settled it in the mid-1600's. Accustomed to an overcrowded, poverty-stricken England that was still recovering from the disastrous effects of a generations-long religious and civil war, the peaceful tranquility of the gentle Maryland countryside must have made many a settler rejoice that his adventuresome spirit led him to leave the Old World for the New. Any of his doubts about leaving home vanished in the face of Maryland's gently rolling land where warm streams rushed through fertile land into Chesapeake Bay and where the forests and marshes teemed with game birds, animals, fish, and shellfish.

The movement of Englishmen to Maryland was inspired by one family, the Calverts of Yorkshire in northern England. After five futile years of trying to

HISTORY AND TRADITIONS OF

maryland

plant a colony in harsh and remote Newfoundland, Lord Calvert appealed to Charles I for another grant to the New World, preferably one closer to the already-established colony of Virginia. He was awarded all the land from present-day Philadelphia to the Potomac, including the entire Chesapeake Bay area. By 1634, the first Maryland colonists had begun the thriving colony of St. Mary's.

Like so many other southern regions, Maryland was tidewater country. Here the streams and rivers that originated in the Appalachians poured into the Atlantic, creating marsh lands that were neither salt nor fresh. These tidewater areas provided an ideal breeding ground for many varieties of seafood. Moreover, they provided nearly every plantation and settlement with an open road to the sea, a means of transporting its produce to England and receiving needed goods in exchange.

Maryland, like its sister colony of Virginia, became a region of tidewater plantations and small towns with a virtually unsettled interior. Huge land grants were issued by the Calverts to men whose dream was the accumulation of a fortune, a fortune they expected to reap by growing tobacco. In these colonies and in Europe, tobacco was literally worth its weight in gold. It was an extraordinarily valuable export crop and moreover, was a medium of exchange within the colony. Many a doctor or lawyer received his fee in pounds of tobacco rather than pounds sterling.

And while her ambitious husband set about clearing and planting his immense land holding, what was the Maryland homemaker doing? Marveling at the abundance around her . . . planning how to use the treasured recipes brought from England with the new foods she was discovering . . . and thriftily planting her kitchen garden with its inevitable border of herbs. How delighted she must have been by the many fresh fish available almost instantly. In England, particularly in northern England that had been home for many of the early Maryland settlers, the only fish available was salted. The tantalizing flavor of fresh fish was a luxury seldom tasted in these homes. And now, in this strange new world, fresh fish was so easily obtained, it could be served almost daily.

One can imagine, too, the excitement generated by the abundance of shell-fish. Great oyster beds lie in the Chesapeake Bay, and here also are found scallops, clams, mussels, and many varieties of crabs. It did not take the enterprising Maryland homemaker long to discover that these shellfish could be served in many tasty dishes. She applied her talents and her "receipts", and thus was born a whole new cuisine.

Springtime in Maryland brings the glory of blooming cherry trees and wild-flowers. But it also signals the arrival of that highly-prized gourmet delight, soft-shell crabs. With such delicious foods available, it was somehow inevitable that Marylanders would have parties featuring these unshelled crustaceans. Thus was born the custom of the springtime soft-shell crab festivals, when huge amounts of these delicacies would be consumed along with plentiful quantities of locally brewed beer, ale, or wine.

Another food custom celebrated springtime, and was set to coincide with Easter. Every family in the district, no matter how busy with spring planting, took time to celebrate Easter in the local church. And following the Easter services came a celebration unique to Maryland. The families would go from home to home, tasting hams. These hams had been prepared days in advance, using carefully-kept secret seasonings. One ham might be boned and rolled around a savory stuffing. Another might be pierced all over with a knife and filled with boiled greens. All the hams would be tasted in one gigantic progressive party. At the end of the day, one family's ham would be declared superior to all others, the champion until the following spring when all the fun and excitement of the competition began again.

After Easter, land-holding Marylanders turned their attention to the matter of clearing land for the crops and protecting that crop until it was ready for harvesting. But with the arrival of autumn, another prized Maryland food appeared on many tables. This food was canvasback duck, a wild game bird that fed on the grains growing in the marshlands along the Maryland coast. When caught and cooked, this bird has a delicate, almost seawater-like flavor that early gourmets were quick to appreciate.

The appreciation of fine foods grown locally was typical of the Maryland people. Later generations would be people who were just as swift to enjoy the land and the fine foods it produced as their ancestors had been. These people would create recipes using those foods, recipes destined to become famous throughout the Deep South and to contribute much to what would one day be a definite Deep South cookery.

EASTERN SHORE CRAB SALAD

1 lb. backfin lump crab meat	3 tbsp. catsup
1 c. finely chopped celery	1 c. salad dressing
2 tbsp. minced green pepper	Juice of 1/2 lemon
1/8 tsp. paprika	1/2 tsp. mustard
1/2 tsp. salt	1 1/2 tbsp. sugar

Combine the crab meat, celery and green pepper in a bowl. Combine the paprika, salt, catsup, salad dressing, lemon juice, mustard and sugar in separate bowl and mix well, then add to the crab meat mixture. Toss lightly until crab meat is well coated. Refrigerate until ready to serve. Serve on lettuce leaf. Garnish with sliced hard-boiled eggs, if desired. 6 servings.

Mrs. Paul Massey, Millington, Maryland

MARTHA WASHINGTON'S CRAB SOUP

2 hard-boiled eggs	1/2 lb. crab meat
1 tbsp. butter	1/2 c. cream
Grated rind of 1 lemon	3/4 c. cooking sherry
1 tbsp. flour	Pepper to taste
1 qt. milk	

Mash the eggs to a paste with a fork, then mix with the butter, lemon rind and flour. Bring the milk to a boil in a saucepan, then add gradually, stirring constantly, to the paste. Return to saucepan. Add the crab meat and simmer for 3 minutes, stirring constantly. Add the cream and sherry and bring to a boil. Season with pepper and serve.

Ruth A. Sale, Charlotte, North Carolina

SAVORY TURTLE SOUP

1 1/2 c. diced fresh turtle meat	3 drops of hot sauce
2 qt. beef stock	1 hard-cooked egg white, diced
1 bay leaf	Salt and pepper to taste
1 clove of mace	Sherry flavoring to taste
1 1/2 tbsp. lemon juice	

Combine the turtle meat, beef stock, bay leaf, mace, lemon juice and hot sauce in a 4-quart saucepan. Bring to a boil, then cook until the turtle meat is tender. Remove the bay leaf and mace, then add the egg white. Season with salt, pepper and sherry flavoring after removing from heat. 8 servings.

Mrs. Georgia McComb, Bethesda, Maryland

South German's White Cabbage Soup (below)

SOUTH GERMAN'S WHITE CABBAGE SOUP

1 head cabbage	1 onion, sliced
2 carrots	1 lb. cubed pork
1 parsnip	5 c. bouillon
4 potatoes	Salt and pepper to taste

Trim and cut the cabbage in pieces. Peel the carrots and cut in quarters. Peel the parsnip and slice. Peel the potatoes and cube. Brown the onion and pork in a small amount of fat in a Dutch oven, then add the bouillon and simmer until the pork is almost tender. Add the remaining ingredients and cook for 30 minutes longer. Serve with French bread and mustard. 4 servings.

CREAMED POTATO SOUP

4 med. potatoes	1 tbsp. butter
1 tsp. salt	1 c. light cream
1 med. onion, chopped	

Peel and cube the potatoes, then place in a large saucepan and add 4 cups water and the salt. Bring to a boil, then cook until tender. Mash the potatoes in the stock. Saute the onion in the butter until transparent, then add to the potatoes. Add the cream and heat thoroughly. 6 servings.

Mrs. Kaye Renfroe, Gaithersbury, Maryland

FRIED SOFT-SHELL CRABS

12 soft-shell crabs	1 c. pancake mix
2 eggs, beaten	1 c. cornmeal
Salt and pepper to taste	Cooking oil
1 tsp. Worcestershire sauce	

Clean the crabs carefully, lifting shell of crab and scooping out on either side, being careful not to break shells. Combine the eggs, salt, pepper and Worcestershire sauce, then dip the crabs in the egg mixture. Coat with the pancake mix, then with the cornmeal. Fry in deep oil at 250 degrees until golden brown.

Mrs. Janice Woolf, Hyattsville, Maryland

DEVILED SCALLOPS

1 qt. scallops, chopped	1/4 tsp. pepper
1 sm. onion, chopped	2 tbsp. flour
1/2 c. melted butter	1 c. scalded milk
1/2 tsp. dry mustard	1/2 c. grated cheese
1/2 tsp. salt	1/2 c. buttered bread crumbs

Combine the scallops, onion and butter in a saucepan and cook for 5 minutes, stirring occasionally. Stir in the mustard, salt, pepper and flour, then add the milk gradually, stirring constantly until thickened. Place in a baking dish and top with the cheese and bread crumbs. Bake at 350 degrees for 20 minutes. 6 servings.

Mrs. Hope Lane, Lanham, Maryland

POACHED PERCH FILLETS

1 1-lb. package frozen perch fillets	5 peppercorns
1 tsp. salt	1 can frozen shrimp soup, thawed
1 tsp. chopped parsley	1/2 c. evaporated milk
1 bay leaf	1/2 tsp. curry powder
1 clove of garlic	1 tsp. lemon juice

Thaw the fillets and separate. Pour 2 cups water in a 10-inch skillet, then add the salt, parsley, bay leaf, garlic and peppercorns and bring to a boil. Add the fillets and bring to a boil. Cover with foil and punch hole in center for steam to escape. Simmer for 10 minutes or until fish flakes easily when tested. Combine the remaining ingredients in a saucepan and simmer, stirring occasionally, until heated through. Remove the fillets with a slotted spoon from skillet and place on a warm platter. Serve the soup mixture over the fillets.

Mrs. John C. Crawford, Jr., Maryville, Tennessee

FESTIVE FILLETS WITH SAUERKRAUT

2 lb. thick fish fillets	1/2 tsp. caraway seed
1 c. chopped onions	1 tsp. salt
1 clove of garlic, minced	1/4 c. flour
2 tbsp. margarine	1/4 c. oil
1 1-lb. 11-oz. can	1 c. sour cream
sauerkraut, drained	1/2 c. shredded Cheddar cheese
1/4 c. dry white wine	2 tbsp. corn flake crumbs

Cut the fillets into 6 portions and refrigerate. Cook the onions and garlic in a heavy 10-inch iron skillet in the margarine until the onions are soft but not brown. Add the sauerkraut, wine, 1/4 cup water and caraway seed, then cover and simmer for 30 minutes or until flavors are blended. Sprinkle the fish with salt and roll in flour. Arrange the fish in a single layer in hot oil in a 10-inch frypan and fry over moderate heat for 4 to 5 minutes or until brown. Turn carefully, then fry for 4 to 5 minutes longer or until fish is lightly browned. Stir the sour cream into the sauerkraut mixture. Arrange the fish over the sauerkraut. Mix the cheese and cornflake crumbs and sprinkle over the fish. Cover tightly with aluminum foil. Bake at 350 degrees for 15 minutes. Uncover and bake for 5 to 10 minutes longer or until fish flakes easily when tested with a fork. Garnish with pimento strips, if desired. 6 servings.

Front: Festive Fillets with Sauerkraut (above)
Back: Oven-Baked Seafood Chowder (page 16)

15

OVEN-BAKED SEAFOOD CHOWDER

2 lb. thick fish fillets	1 sm. bay leaf
2 c. sliced carrots	1/4 c. butter or margarine
2 c. cubed potatoes	1/2 c. dry white wine (opt.)
2 c. sliced onions	1 c. half and half
2 tsp. salt	2 tbsp. flour
1 tsp. dillweed	2 tbsp. chopped parsley
2 whole cloves	

Cut the fish into 1 1/2-inch pieces and refrigerate. Combine the carrots, potatoes, onions, salt, dillweed, cloves, bay leaf and butter in a 6-quart ovenproof Dutch oven. Add 2 cups boiling water and cover tightly. Bake at 375 degrees for 40 minutes or until vegetables are tender. Add the fish and the wine, then cover and cook for 20 minutes longer or until the fish flakes easily when tested with a fork. Remove from oven. Combine the half and half and flour and blend until smooth. Add to the chowder and heat, stirring carefully until slightly thickened. Garnish with the parsley. 10 cups chowder.

Photograph for this recipe on page 15.

STUFFED FLOUNDER

1 2-lb. flounder, cleaned	3 slices toast, cubed
3 tbsp. lemon juice	2 eggs
3 tbsp. chopped parsley	Salt and pepper to taste
1 onion, minced	1 1/2 c. crab meat
1 clove of garlic, minced	1/4 c. Parmesan cheese
1/2 green pepper, minced	Paprika
1/4 c. butter	

Cut a slit to the bone down dark side of flounder. Pour the lemon juice in the slit, then stuff with the parsley. Marinate in the refrigerator for 2 hours. Saute the onion, garlic and green pepper in the butter until soft, then combine with the remaining ingredients except the cheese and paprika. Remove the parsley from the flounder and stuff with crab meat mixture. Place in baking pan. Bake in 375-degree oven for about 45 minutes, then sprinkle with the cheese and paprika. Bake for about 15 minutes longer. 4 servings.

Mrs. Mabel B. Breen, Galveston, Texas

MARYLAND CRAB CAKES

2 eggs, well beaten	1 tsp. Worcestershire sauce
2 tbsp. mayonnaise	3 c. crab meat
Salt and pepper to taste	Flour

Combine all the ingredients except the flour in a bowl and mix lightly. Add enough flour to handle easily, then shape into patties. Dust lightly with flour. Fry in a small amount of fat until browned on both sides. 4 servings.

Mrs. Lillian B. Gardner, Tampa, Florida

CRAB IMPERIAL

2 lb. crab meat	1 tbsp. dry mustard
1 green pepper, minced	3 tbsp. mayonnaise
2 pimentos, diced	2 eggs, beaten
1/3 tsp. salt	3 tbsp. sherry
1/2 tsp. white pepper	Paprika

Combine all the ingredients except the paprika and mix well. Place in a baking dish and spread with additional mayonnaise. Sprinkle with paprika. Bake at 350 degrees for 25 minutes or until heated and bubbly. 4-6 servings.

Mrs. Melvin J. Abrams, Baltimore, Maryland

BAKED BLUEFISH

1 bluefish, cleaned	1 bay leaf
1 tbsp. minced scallion stems	Salt and pepper to taste
1 tbsp. butter	Thyme to taste
1 c. white wine	

Place the bluefish in a shallow baking dish. Saute the scallion stems in butter, then add the wine, bay leaf, salt and pepper and thyme. Bring to a boil, then pour over the bluefish. Bake in 425-degree oven until fish flakes easily when tested with a fork. Do not overbake.

Mrs. Patsy Smith, Silver Spring, Maryland

SHRIMP HARPIN

2 1/2 lb. large shelled shrimp, deveined	1 tsp. salt
1 tbsp. lemon juice	1/8 tsp. pepper
1 tbsp. salad oil	1/8 tsp. mace
3/4 c. rice	Dash of cayenne pepper
1/4 c. minced green pepper	1 c. heavy cream
1/4 c. minced onion	1 c. sherry
2 tbsp. butter	3/4 c. slivered almonds

Preheat the oven to 350 degrees. Cook the shrimp in boiling salted water for 5 minutes, then drain. Reserve 8 shrimp for garnish. Place the remaining shrimp in a 2-quart casserole and sprinkle with lemon juice and salad oil. Cook the rice according to package directions. Saute the green pepper and onion in the butter in a skillet for 5 minutes, then add with the rice, salt, pepper, mace, cayenne pepper, cream, sherry and 1/2 cup almonds to shrimp in the casserole. Toss well. Bake, uncovered, for 35 minutes. Top with the reserved shrimp and the remaining almonds and bake for 20 minutes longer. 6-8 servings.

Margaret Hudson, Jackson, Mississippi

EASY LOBSTER CURRY

1 pkg. frozen lobster
1 1/2 tsp. curry powder
1 tbsp. sherry
2 cans cream of chicken soup

3/4 can evaporated milk
1/2 tsp. sugar
Salt and pepper to taste

Cook the lobster according to package directions and cut into small pieces. Combine with the remaining ingredients, then place in a baking dish. Bake in 325-degree oven for 30 minutes. Serve with rice. 4 servings.

Mrs. Elsie Crocker, Cumberland, Maryland

OYSTER PIE SUPREME

1 pt. select oysters
1 recipe pastry for 2-crust
    pie

Juice of 1 lemon
Butter
Freshly ground pepper to taste

Drain the oysters and place in a pastry-lined pie plate. Sprinkle with lemon juice and dot generously with butter. Sprinkle with pepper. Cover with pastry, then cut steam vents and crimp edges. Bake at 425 degrees for 20 minutes or until crust is brown.

Mrs. Alyce Tincher, Anthony, Texas

SAUERBRATEN

1 4-lb. beef rump roast
Salt to taste
1 tsp. freshly ground pepper
1 onion, sliced
3 bay leaves
Peppercorns

2 c. vinegar
1 tbsp. sugar
2 tbsp. shortening
12 gingersnaps, crumbled
1 c. sour cream

Sprinkle the roast with salt and pepper and rub in thoroughly. Place in a deep bowl. Add the onion, bay leaves and peppercorns. Combine 2 cups water, vinegar and sugar in a saucepan and bring to a boil. Pour over the roast to cover. Cover bowl tightly. Refrigerate for 3 to 4 days, turning occasionally. Remove from the marinade and reserve the marinade, then pat the roast dry. Brown on all sides in the shortening in a Dutch oven. Add 1 cup of the reserved marinade, then cover and simmer until tender, adding marinade as needed. Remove the roast to a warm platter. Add 2 cups reserved marinade to the pan dripping and season with salt, then stir in the gingersnaps. Heat thoroughly, stirring constantly, then stir in the sour cream. Serve with the roast.

Mrs. Wright L. Spradlin, Eva, Oklahoma

Corned Beef Quiche (below)

CORNED BEEF QUICHE

1 unbaked 9-in. pie shell	1/4 tsp. salt
1 15-oz. can corned beef	Dash of nutmeg
hash	2 eggs, beaten
1 c. shredded Swiss cheese	1 1/4 c. milk
2 tsp. flour	

Bake the pie shell at 450 degrees for 7 minutes, then remove from the oven. Reduce the oven temperature to 325 degrees. Crumble the corned beef hash into pie shell. Top with the cheese. Combine the remaining ingredients and pour over hash and cheese. Bake for 35 to 40 minutes or until set. Cool for 25 minutes before serving.

BRISKET OF BEEF WITH SAUERKRAUT AND DUMPLINGS

2 tbsp. shortening	1 onion, sliced
1 3-lb. brisket of beef	2 cans sauerkraut
Salt and pepper to taste	1 recipe dumpling dough

Melt the shortening in a large skillet. Season the brisket with salt and pepper and place in the skillet. Add the onion and cook until brisket and onion are browned. Add the sauerkraut and cover with boiling water. Cook over low heat for 2 hours or until brisket is tender. Roll out the dough on a floured surface and cut into squares. Place on brisket and cover. Cook for 25 minutes and serve immediately.

Vergie V. Kahla, Port Bolivar, Texas

English Harvest Lamb Stew (below)

ENGLISH HARVEST LAMB STEW

4 lb. lamb neck slices
2 tbsp. salad oil
1   13-3/4 oz. can chicken
    broth
2 tsp. salt
1/4 tsp. pepper
2 tsp. oregano leaves
1/2 tsp. thyme leaves
1/2 tsp. nutmeg
1 clove of garlic, minced

2 c. diced white turnips
1 c. sliced carrots
12 sm. white onions
1 med. green pepper, cut in
    1 in. strips
2 tbsp. flour
1   8-oz. can whole kernel
    corn
Chopped chives to taste

Brown the lamb in hot oil in a Dutch oven, then pour off the fat. Add the broth, 2 cups water and seasonings and bring to a boil. Cover and simmer for about 1 hour or until lamb is tender. Skim off the fat from the broth. Add the turnips, carrots, onions and green pepper, then cook, covered, for about 20 minutes or until the vegetables are almost tender. Blend the flour with 1/4 cup water and add the corn and flour mixture to the stew. Cook, uncovered, for about 10 minutes longer, or until heated through, stirring frequently. Sprinkle with chives before serving.

HASENPFEFFER

1/2 lb. lean bacon, diced
1   5-lb. rabbit, disjointed
1/2 tsp. salt

1/2 tsp. freshly ground pepper
1/2 c. flour
1/2 c. minced shallots

1/2 tsp. minced garlic
1 c. dry red wine
1 c. chicken stock
2 tbsp. brandy
1 tsp. currant jelly

1 sm. bay leaf
1/8 tsp. dried rosemary
1/8 tsp. dried thyme
2 tsp. fresh lemon juice

Fry the bacon over moderate heat in a Dutch oven, stirring and turning frequently until crisp. Remove the bacon and drain on a paper towel. Sprinkle the rabbit with salt and pepper, then dip in the flour, shaking off the excess. Add the rabbit, several pieces at a time, to the bacon drippings and brown on all sides quickly and evenly. Remove to a plate. Saute the shallots and garlic in 2 tablespoons of the drippings for 4 to 5 minutes or until shallots are transparent. Pour in the wine and the stock, then bring to a boil, scraping brown bits from bottom of pan. Stir in the brandy, jelly, bay leaf, rosemary and thyme. Return the rabbit to the Dutch oven, then add the bacon. Cover tightly and simmer for 1 hour and 30 minutes or until the rabbit is tender. Remove the rabbit to a heated platter, then remove the bay leaf and stir in the lemon juice. Season with additional salt and pepper if needed. Sauce should be peppery. Pour the sauce over the rabbit. 6 servings.

Mrs. James Michael Segrest, Tuscaloosa, Alabama

PORK CHOPS AND SAUERKRAUT

4 end pork chops
2 med. onions, chopped
1 No. 2 1/2 can sauerkraut,
    drained
1/8 tsp. pepper

Dash of cayenne pepper
1 1/2 c. water
8 med. potatoes
1 tbsp. caraway seed
1 tsp. salt

Brown the pork chops on both sides over low heat in a large kettle, then remove chops. Add onions to fat remaining in kettle and cook for 5 minutes, stirring occasionally. Add the sauerkraut, pepper, cayenne pepper and water and stir well. Place the potatoes and chops on sauerkraut mixture and sprinkle with caraway seed and salt. Bring to a boil and cover. Simmer for about 1 hour. 4 servings.

Mrs. Theodore Wolfe, Tunnelton, West Virginia

SAUSAGE-EGG SCRAMBLE

1 lb. bulk pork sausage
5 eggs

1/2 c. milk
Salt and pepper to taste

Brown the sausage in a skillet, stirring frequently. Drain off the fat. Combine the eggs, milk, salt and pepper in a bowl and beat until blended. Pour over the sausage and cook over low heat, stirring frequently, until the eggs are soft but set. Yield: 4 servings.

Cleo P. Wright, Greensburg, Kentucky

SAUSAGE AND BROCCOLI CASSEROLE

1/2 lb. bulk sausage	2 pkg. chopped cooked broccoli
1/2 c. minced onion	1/2 tsp. salt
3 tbsp. milk or cream	1/4 tsp. nutmeg
3 eggs, beaten	1/4 c. bread crumbs

Shape the sausage in small balls and brown with onion in a skillet. Stir in milk and eggs. Add broccoli, salt and nutmeg and pour into a casserole. Top with bread crumbs. Bake at 350 degrees for 30 minutes or until browned. Serve with cheese sauce, if desired.

Mrs. Andrew J. Hillman, Fordyce, Arkansas

SUCCULENT MUTTON DISH

3 1/2 lb. boned mutton shoulder	1 sm. can tomato paste
1/4 c. fat	2 sprigs of parsley
1 tsp. sugar	2 sprigs of thyme
Salt and pepper to taste	1/2 bay leaf
3 tbsp. flour	2 lb. small potatoes, pared
3 pt. boiling water	10 button onions
1 clove of garlic, minced	

Cut the mutton into cubes. Heat the fat in a saucepan and add the mutton and sugar. Brown the mutton well and season with salt and pepper. Stir in the flour and cook, stirring constantly, until the flour browns. Add the water slowly, stirring constantly. Add the garlic, tomato paste, parsley, thyme and bay leaf and bring to boiling point. Cover the saucepan and simmer the mutton mixture for 1 hour. Remove mutton and cool the sauce. Remove any grease from the top of sauce. Place the mutton in a large casserole and strain sauce over the mutton. Place potatoes over the mutton. Saute the onions in 2 tablespoons additional fat in a saucepan and drain. Add the onions to casserole and cover casserole tightly. Bake in 350-degree oven for 1 hour. 8 servings.

Mrs. Peter Wiese, Birmingham, Alabama

FRICASSEE OF CHICKEN

2 2 1/2 to 3-lb. fryers	4 ripe tomatoes
Salt and pepper to taste	2 tsp. paprika
1/4 lb. butter or margarine	3 c. thin cream
2 med. onions, finely chopped	1/8 tsp. soda

Cut the chickens in serving pieces and sprinkle with salt and pepper. Melt the butter in a large frying pan or Dutch oven. Add the onions and place the chicken over onions. Cover. Cook over low heat for 10 minutes. Peel and chop the tomatoes and add to the chicken mixture. Add the paprika and stir lightly. Cook for 10 minutes. Mix the cream with soda and pour over chicken mixture. Cover and cook for 35 minutes or until chicken is tender. Remove chicken to platter. Strain the sauce and pour over the chicken. 6-8 servings.

Mrs. Inez Freed, Fort Worth, Texas

CHICKEN A LA MARYLAND

1/4 c. flour	1 egg, well beaten
2 tsp. salt	1 1/2 c. fine dry bread crumbs
1 3-lb. chicken, disjointed	2 tbsp. butter or margarine

Combine the flour and the salt, then dredge the chicken with the flour mixture. Dip in the egg, then roll in the crumbs. Place in a greased baking dish and dot with the butter, then cover. Bake at 350 degrees for about 1 hour. Remove the cover and bake until the chicken is tender and browned. 6 servings.

Mrs. Tracy Todd, Westminster, Maryland

MARINATED CHARCOAL CHICKEN

1 c. Italian dressing	Lemon juice to taste
1/2 c. vinegar	Salt and pepper to taste
1/2 c. sherry	2 2 1/2-lb. broilers,
Dash of Worcestershire sauce	quartered

Combine all the ingredients except the chicken in a deep bowl. Add the chicken and marinate in the refrigerator for at least 12 hours, turning occasionally. Remove the chicken from the marinade and place on grill over low coals. Cook until tender, turning and basting with the marinade. 8 servings.

Mrs. S. S. Helmly, Monk's Corner, South Carolina

GOLDEN CRUNCH-FRIED CHICKEN

1 2 1/2-lb. chicken	1/2 tsp. pepper
1 c. flour	1 c. buttermilk
2 tsp. salt	1/2 tsp. soda

Disjoint the chicken and remove the skin. Combine the flour, salt and pepper in a paper bag, then add 1 piece of chicken at a time and shake until well coated. Combine the buttermilk and soda in a bowl, then dip the chicken in the buttermilk and shake in the flour mixture again. Fry in deep fat at 350 degrees for about 20 minutes or until tender and brown. Drain on absorbent paper. 6 servings.

Mrs. Homer Cross, Camden, Arkansas

Roast Turkey with Tropical Rice Stuffing (below)

ROAST TURKEY WITH TROPICAL RICE STUFFING

1 13 1/2-oz. can pineapple tidbits	1 5-oz. can water chestnuts, sliced
1 10 1/2-oz. can chicken consomme	1/2 c. chopped green onion
1 c. rice	1/2 c. thinly sliced celery
1/4 c. butter	1 tbsp. soy sauce
	1 10-lb. turkey

Drain the syrup from pineapple and combine with the consomme. Measure and add enough water to make 2 cups. Stir in the rice and bring to a boil. Cover and cook for 15 minutes. Mix in the pineapple and the remaining ingredients except turkey. Stuff in neck and body cavities of turkey. Secure with skewers. Wrap in foil and place in baking pan. Bake at 400 degrees for 3 hours and 15 minutes. Turn down foil and baste with drippings. Bake for 30 minutes longer, basting frequently.

QUAIL PIE

6 quail, cleaned	3 tbsp. cornstarch
Salt and pepper to taste	1 recipe biscuits

Place the quail in a saucepan and cover with 3 cups water. Season with salt and pepper. Simmer until tender. Remove the quail from broth and cool, then remove the meat from the bones. Mix the cornstarch with small amount of water and stir into the broth. Bring to a boil, then reduce the heat and simmer, stirring constantly, until broth is thickened. Add the quail meat and turn into a baking dish. Top with the biscuits. Bake at 450 degrees for 12 minutes or until biscuits are browned. 6 servings.

Mrs. Wynola Henderson, Cumberland, Maryland

MALLARD DUCK WITH BING CHERRIES

2 tbsp. butter	2 tsp. potato flour or
1 4-lb. mallard duck	cornstarch
2 tbsp. dry sherry	1 tsp. tomato paste
1/4 tsp. crushed garlic	1/2 bay leaf
1 can pitted Bing cherries	

Heat the butter in a skillet. Cut the duck in quarters and brown in the butter. Drain off fat and pour sherry over duck. Remove duck to a casserole. Add garlic to same skillet. Drain the cherries and reserve juice. Place the cherries in skillet and cook for 2 minutes. Blend potato flour with reserved cherry juice and tomato paste and add to cherries. Cook, stirring constantly, until thickened. Pour over duck and add bay leaf. Cover. Bake at 350 degrees for about 45 minutes or until duck is done. 4 servings.

Mrs. Martin Gobel, Baltimore, Maryland

COOKED FRESH BROCCOLI

2 1/2 lb. fresh broccoli	3 tbsp. butter
Salt and pepper to taste	

Wash the broccoli and split the thick heads. Place the broccoli in boiling, salted water with the ends down and the heads out of the water. Cook for 10 to 20 minutes or until stem ends are tender. Push the heads under the water and cook for 5 minutes longer. Drain. Season with salt, pepper and butter. Broccoli may be served with white or hollandaise sauce. 6-8 servings.

Mrs. J. E. Shirey, Spring Lake, Texas

HOMINY IN SOUR CREAM

2 cans golden hominy	1 c. sour cream
2 tbsp. chunk butter	Salt and pepper to taste

Drain and rinse the hominy. Melt the butter in a skillet, then add the hominy. Cover with the sour cream and season with salt and pepper. Simmer, stirring frequently, until heated through. Serve with ham.

Mrs. Jacky Bridges, Pendleton, South Carolina

Lamb-Stuffed Cabbage (below)

LAMB-STUFFED CABBAGE

1 lge. head cabbage	2 8-oz. cans tomato sauce
1 1/2 lb. lean ground lamb	1 6-oz. can tomato paste
1/2 c. fine dry bread crumbs	2 tbsp. lemon juice
2 tbsp. minced onion	2 tbsp. sugar
1 egg	Raisin Rice
Salt and pepper	

Cook the cabbage for 3 minutes in boiling water in a large kettle, then cool. Combine the lamb, bread crumbs, onion, egg, 1 teaspoon salt and 1/4 teaspoon pepper and mix well. Separate the leaves of the cabbage and use about 18 of the outer leaves. Place a small amount of lamb mixture in each leaf, then roll and secure with a wooden pick. Combine the tomato sauce, tomato paste, 1 cup water, lemon juice, sugar and salt and pepper to taste in a large kettle, then add the stuffed cabbage. Simmer, covered, for 1 hour and 30 minutes. Serve with Raisin Rice.

Raisin Rice

1 c. rice	1/8 tsp. grated lemon peel
1/2 c. raisins	

Cook the rice according to package directions, adding the raisins and lemon peel.

GERMAN RED CABBAGE

1 head red cabbage	1/2 c. currant jelly
1/4 lb. butter	1 bay leaf
2 onions, sliced	Salt and pepper to taste
2 cored apples, sliced	1/3 c. vinegar

Shred the cabbage coarsely. Melt the butter in a large heavy saucepan, then add all the ingredients except the vinegar. Add 1/4 cup water, then cover and bring to a boil. Reduce the heat and simmer for 2 hours, stirring occasionally. Remove the bay leaf and stir in the vinegar. 6 servings.

Mrs. Hugh Kossoff, Danville, Virginia

ASPARAGUS-CRAB CASSEROLE

2 tbsp. butter	1 tsp. salt
2 tbsp. flour	1/8 tsp. pepper
1 2/3 c. milk	30 cooked asparagus spears
1/4 c. grated sharp Cheddar	1/2 lb. crab meat
cheese	Grated Parmesan cheese
1/4 c. grated Swiss cheese	

Melt the butter in a saucepan, then stir in the flour. Add the milk gradually, stirring constantly, to make a smooth sauce. Add the Cheddar and Swiss cheeses and stir until melted. Add the seasonings and simmer for 10 minutes longer. Line a 2-quart baking dish with asparagus and sprinkle with additional salt and pepper. Place a layer of crab meat over the asparagus and cover with the sauce. Sprinkle heavily with Parmesan cheese. Bake at 375 degrees for about 20 minutes. 8-10 servings.

Mrs. James L. Glymp, Baltimore, Maryland

CREAMED NEW POTATOES AND PEAS

8 sm. new potatoes, scraped	1 4-oz. carton whipped
1 1/2 c. shelled English peas	cream cheese with chives
Salt	1/4 c. milk
1/2 tsp. sugar	

Cook the potatoes in salted water for 15 to 20 minutes, then drain. Cook the peas in a small amount of boiling water till tender, adding 1/2 teaspoon salt and the sugar, then drain the peas. Blend the cream cheese, milk and 1/4 teaspoon salt together in a saucepan and heat, stirring, over low heat just until warm. Combine the hot potatoes and peas in a serving dish and pour the cream cheese sauce over the vegetables. 4-6 servings.

Mrs. Arthur A. Behrens, San Saba, Texas

FRENCH-FRIED EGGPLANT

1 eggplant	2 tbsp. milk
1 egg, beaten	1 c. seasoned flour

Peel the eggplant and cut into strips. Place in salted ice water in refrigerator for at least 1 hour, then remove and drain. Combine the egg and milk in a bowl. Dip the eggplant in the flour, then into the egg mixture and coat with the flour again. Fry in deep fat at 375 degrees for 3 or 4 minutes or until browned. 4 servings.

Mrs. Eunice Taylor, Eufaula, Alabama

CORN BREAD MUFFINS

1/2 c. cornmeal	2 tsp. baking powder
1/2 c. flour	1 egg, beaten
2 tbsp. sugar	1/2 c. milk
1/2 tsp. salt	2 tbsp. bacon drippings

Sift the dry ingredients together into a bowl, then add the remaining ingredients. Stir until well blended. Fill greased muffin cups 2/3 full with batter. Bake at 425 degrees for 15 minutes or until browned. 8 muffins.

Mrs. Albert Minson, Vinita, Oklahoma

MARYLAND BEATEN BISCUITS

5 c. all-purpose flour	1/2 tsp. baking powder
2 tsp. salt	1 c. lard

Combine all the ingredients except lard in a mixing bowl and cut in the lard, then add enough water to make a stiff dough. Knead until dough holds together, then place on a heavy table or block and beat with a hammer for 30 minutes or until dough blisters. Shape into small biscuits and place on a baking sheet. Bake at 400 degrees for 25 to 30 minutes. 35-40 biscuits.

Thelma Arthur, Smyrna, Delaware

IRISH SODA BREAD

4 c. flour	1/2 c. margarine
3/4 c. sugar	2 c. seedless raisins
3 tsp. baking powder	2 tbsp. caraway seed (opt.)
1 tsp. soda	2 c. buttermilk
1 tsp. salt	

Mix the dry ingredients in a bowl and cut in the margarine until mixture is crumbly. Stir in the raisins and caraway seed, then buttermilk. Place in 2 well-greased 9 x 5-inch loaf pans. Bake at 325 degrees for 1 hour. Slice thin and spread with cream cheese, if desired.

Mrs. John Biddle, Mayport, Florida

CINNAMON BRAID

2 pkg. yeast	1 c. milk, scalded
1/4 c. warm water	5 c. (about) flour
Sugar	2 eggs
2 tsp. salt	4 tbsp. melted butter
1/4 c. shortening	Cinnamon

Dissolve the yeast in warm water. Mix 1/2 cup sugar, salt, shortening and milk in a large bowl and cool to lukewarm. Add half the flour and mix well. Add yeast and eggs and beat well. Add enough flour to make a soft dough and knead until smooth and satiny. Place in a bowl and cover. Let rise until doubled in bulk. Punch down and let rest for 10 minutes. Place 2 tablespoons melted butter, 1 tablespoon sugar and 1 tablespoon water each in two 4 1/2 x 8 1/2-inch loaf pans. Divide dough in half. Divide each half into 3 parts and roll each part into 20-inch long strips. Roll in cinnamon and braid 3 strips together. Tuck under ends and fit in loaf pans. Brush tops with additional milk and sprinkle with cinnamon and sugar. Let rise until doubled in bulk. Bake at 375 degrees for 35 minutes.

Mrs. R. L. Flurry, Ocean Springs, Mississippi

CHERRY BAKEWELL TART

1 unbaked 9-in. pie shell	1/8 tsp. salt
1 8-oz. jar red maraschino cherries	3/4 c. sugar
	1/3 c. flour
1/3 c. apricot preserves	1/4 c. toasted filberts, chopped
1 tsp. grated lemon peel	
2 tbsp. lemon juice	1/2 c. heavy cream, whipped
4 eggs, separated	

Bake the pie shell at 400 degrees for 10 minutes, then cool slightly. Drain the cherries and slice, reserving 6 for garnish. Mix the sliced cherries with the preserves, lemon peel and juice. Spread over bottom of pie shell. Beat the egg whites with the salt until stiff but not dry. Combine the egg yolks and sugar and beat until thick and lemon colored. Stir in the flour and filberts, then fold in the egg whites. Pour into the pie shell. Bake at 350 degrees for 45 minutes or until toothpick inserted in center comes out clean. Cool thoroughly away from drafts. Garnish with whipped cream and reserved cherries.

Cherry Bakewell Tart (above)

SOUTHERN SYLLABUB

2 c. cream	2 c. milk
1/2 c. sugar	1/2 c. bourbon

Combine all the ingredients in a large deep bowl. Beat with a rotary beater until foamy, then skim off the foam and place in glasses. Continue beating and skimming until all the mixture is used.

Mrs. Karen White, Danville, Virginia

EGG CUSTARD PIE

5 eggs	1 tsp. nutmeg
2 c. sugar	1 tsp. flour
1 qt. milk	2 unbaked pie shells
1 tsp. vanilla	

Beat the eggs and add the sugar, mixing thoroughly. Add the milk, vanilla, nutmeg and flour and blend well. Pour into the pie shells. Bake at 375 degrees for 25 to 30 minutes or until custard is set.

Mrs. P. W. Robertson, Spray, North Carolina

BUTTERSCOTCH MERINGUE PIE

5 tbsp. sifted flour	2 eggs, separated
2/3 c. (packed) light brown sugar	1 tsp. vanilla
3 tbsp. butter or margarine	1 baked pie shell
1 1/2 c. milk	1/4 c. sugar

Combine the flour, brown sugar and butter in top of a double boiler and mix well. Stir in the milk and cook over boiling water until thickened, stirring constantly. Stir small amount of milk mixture into beaten egg yolks. Stir back into the milk mixture and cook for 10 minutes longer, stirring frequently. Add the vanilla and cool. Pour into the pie shell. Beat the egg whites in a bowl until stiff, adding sugar gradually. Spread over filling. Bake at 400 degrees for 8 to 10 minutes or until light brown.

Mrs. Avery Lawing, Newton, North Carolina

LADY BALTIMORE CAKE

3/4 c. butter	1 c. milk
2 c. sugar	1 tsp. lemon extract
3 1/2 tsp. baking powder	8 egg whites, stiffly beaten
3 1/2 c. flour	

Cream the butter in a large mixing bowl, then add the sugar gradually. Sift the baking powder and flour together 3 times, then add to the creamed mixture alternately with milk. Add the lemon extract and fold in the egg whites. Spoon the batter evenly into 3 greased and floured layer cake pans. Bake at 350 degrees until cake tests done. Cool.

Icing

3 c. sugar	1/2 c. diced candied cherries
3 egg whites, stiffly beaten	1 c. chopped nuts
1 c. chopped citron	1 tsp. lemon juice
1 c. chopped raisins	

Combine the sugar and 1 cup boiling water in a saucepan and stir until the sugar is dissolved. Boil, without stirring, until the syrup spins a thread. Pour the syrup slowly over the egg whites, beating constantly, until stiff. Continue beating until icing is cool, then add the fruits, nuts and lemon juice. Spread between layers and over the cake.

Mrs. R. E. Chappell, Dothan, Alabama

RASPBERRY BOMBE

5/8 c. sugar	1 c. cream, whipped
5/8 c. water	1 tbsp. grated orange rind
5 egg yolks	1 tbsp. Grand Marnier
2 pt. raspberry ice cream	1 egg white, stiffly beaten

Mix the sugar and water in a saucepan and bring to a boil. Cook, stirring constantly, to 217 degrees on a candy thermometer. Remove from heat and cool. Beat egg yolks in the top of a double boiler until light and creamy, then place over boiling water. Add syrup gradually, stirring constantly, until well mixed. Cook, stirring constantly, until thick. Remove from heat and set top of double boiler in a pan of cold water. Stir until cold. Line a chilled mold with ice cream to 3/4-inch thickness, then freeze. Combine whipped cream, orange rind and Grand Marnier and beat into egg yolk mixture slowly. Fold in egg white and pour into the ice cream-lined mold. Freeze. Remove from freezer and let stand for several minutes. Turn out onto serving dish. Vanilla or cognac may be substituted for Grand Marnier. 6-8 servings.

Mrs. Arthur King, Richmond, Virginia

RASPBERRY MOUSSELINE

1 qt. fresh raspberries	1 tsp. vanilla
1 tbsp. lemon juice	1 1/2 c. heavy cream, whipped
3/4 c. sugar	Whole strawberries
2 env. unflavored gelatin	Ladyfingers (opt.)

Crush the raspberries and mash through a sieve. Mix the puree, lemon juice and sugar until sugar is dissolved. Soften the gelatin in 1/2 cup water and dissolve over hot water. Add to the raspberry mixture with vanilla. Chill until thickened. Fold in the whipped cream and pour into a 1 1/2-quart mold rinsed in cold water. Chill until firm. Unmold onto a large serving plate and garnish with strawberries. Split the ladyfingers and arrange around sides of the mold. 8 servings.

Marie Bedsole, Alexandria, Louisiana

favorite foods of the virginias

There are two Virginias, each one with its own distinct history, traditions, and ways of preparing food. There is Tidewater Virginia with its tidy settlements and sprawling riverside plantations. This Virginia is characterized by such distinctly English foods as Roast Beef and Yorkshire Pudding, Sally Lunn, and Williamsburg Orange-Wine Cake. Families in this part of the Virginias could and did proudly trace ancestors back to the courts of England.

Further west, where the James and Potomac rivers rise in the Blue Ridge Mountains and a narrow valley separates those mountains from the rest of the Alleghenies lies another Virginia. That one is typified by such foods as Brunswick Stew, Smithfield Ham, and Southern Spoon Bread.

But for all their differences, the two Virginias are both part of the Deep South. One serves to remind the rest of the region of its past and to maintain cherished traditions that might otherwise have been lost. The other provided a jumping-off point for settlements throughout the rest of the Deep South. From Virginia's mountain communities, brave men and women moved down the Shenandoah Valley and through mountain gaps until the entire region as far west as Louisiana had been settled.

Come now, and discover the two worlds of Virginia by tasting the time-honored recipes in this section that follows.

Of the two Virginias, by far the longer settled is the rolling countryside that borders on the Atlantic. Here wide flat rivers roll down into the ocean, forming miles of tidewater flats similar to those found along Maryland's Chesapeake Bay — and just as productive of edible wildlife and seafood. John Smith, prominent among the early settlers of Virginia, described the region as a place where "mountains, hills, plains, valleys, rivers, and brooks all run most pleasantly into a fair bay compassed but for the mouth with fruitful and delightsome land."

Smith was writing his words of praise to encourage settlement of the region, but he was exaggerating neither its beauty nor its fruitfulness. English colonists who flocked to Virginia found the first few years — the "starving time"

HISTORY AND TRADITIONS OF
the virginias

— hard going. But after that, the fertile land yielded its abundance, and great manorial houses began to appear along the James and Potomac rivers. With the manorial houses came long distances between neighbors and an ensuing tradition of hospitality. After all, when people lived far apart, they were quick to welcome not only neighbors but strangers who might bring news of the outside world.

This evolving tradition of hospitality was given impetus by events in far-off England. There in the mid-1600's, when the Virginia colony was forty years old and well-established, the King's supporters lost a civil war. These supporters, called "cavaliers" fled by the thousands to the New World. Many of them settled around the Virginia colony where their friends and relatives had previously built up prosperous land holdings. These newcomers established homes where the gracious traditions of the English court life were preserved, cherished, and handed down to succeeding generations. Among the most highly regarded of these traditions was an ancient one demanding that complete hospitality belonged to the visitor in one's home. So it was that in Virginia certain customs emerged. There would be great house parties lasting for weeks on end ... hunt breakfasts ... elegant balls where beautifully gowned ladies and gentlemen in wigs and knee pants danced the minuet — in short, Virginia developed all the customs and traditions of people who rejoiced in meeting and sharing experiences with each other.

One of these delightful shared experiences was a good dinner, and in the 1700's, people all over Virginia knew that some of the finest food anywhere appeared on Thomas Jefferson's table at Monticello. Jefferson had been the colonies' ambassador to the French court and while there had apprenticed his cook to a great French chef. Moreover, Jefferson was also a man of many scientific talents, including one for botany. He grew many varieties of fruits and vegetables at Monticello. The combination of classic French cuisine and tasty fresh fruits and vegetables produced some of the most memorable meals in the memory of any Virginian.

WEST VIRGINIA

While Virginia was developing a society that emulated the English court and evolved its own gracious traditions, miles to the west a new kind of settlement was being created. Here lived the frontiersmen or mountain men, fiercely independent people whose delight in life was to explore the wilds of the Appalachian Mountains. Many of these people had been indentured servants in Virginia and Maryland . . . when their period of service expired, they headed west with a horse, supplies, and perhaps a wife. They found a hollow or plateau, and there they cleared the land for a small farm. These were the yeomen farmers, and the foods that appeared on their tables were very different from those of Virginia.

Here could be found a dish now traditional throughout most of the South, Brunswick Stew. Small game animals such as rabbit, squirrel, or opossum would be cooked until the meat came away from the bones and was fork-tender. Available vegetables and seasonings would be added, and the result was a hearty dish, filling and nutritious enough to carry a hard-working mountain family through a day of hunting and farming.

Like their Virginia neighbors, the West Virginians also developed a tradition of hospitality. Strangers were their one link with the world. The itinerant preacher or peddlar not only brought spiritual solace or needed goods, he also brought precious news and gossip. So it was that Virginia and West Virginia, seemingly different on the surface, developed a common tradition of hospitality, a tradition we are to find emerging again and again as we explore the history and customs of the South.

English Cheddar Soup with Olives (below)

ENGLISH CHEDDAR SOUP WITH OLIVES

5 slices bacon	3 c. shredded sharp Cheddar cheese
1/2 c. grated carrot	1 4-3/4-oz. jar pimento-
1/2 c. chopped celery	stuffed olives
1/2 c. chopped onion	2 c. milk
1/2 c. chopped green pepper	2 tbsp. dry sherry
1/4 c. flour	Coarsely ground pepper to taste
4 c. chicken broth	1 tbsp. chopped parsley

Cook the bacon until crisp in a Dutch oven, then drain on paper towels and crumble. Saute the carrot, celery, onion and green pepper in the bacon drippings over low heat for about 5 minutes or until crisp tender. Do not brown. Blend in the flour, then stir in chicken broth gradually. Cook over low heat, stirring constantly, until mixture thickens and boils, then simmer for 5 minutes. Add cheese and stir over low heat until the cheese is melted. Drain the olives and slice. Stir in milk, sherry and olives and simmer for 10 minutes. Season with pepper. Serve garnished with crumbled bacon and parsley.

BRUNSWICK STEW

1 5-lb. hen	Red pepper and salt to taste
3 No. 2 cans tomatoes	3 lb. cooked potatoes, mashed
1 8-oz. can tomato paste	2 No. 2 cans corn
2 No. 2 cans cut okra	1 stick butter or margarine
3 lge. onions, minced	

Cook the chicken in boiling water until tender. Remove chicken from broth and cool. Remove chicken from bones and place in broth. Add the tomatoes, tomato paste, okra, onions, pepper and salt and cook over low heat for about 2 hours. Add the potatoes and corn and cook for 15 minutes longer, stirring occasionally. Add the butter. May be cooked longer to improve flavor. May be frozen.

Mrs. E. C. Henry, Canton, Mississippi

OYSTER STEW

1 c. light cream	1 tsp. celery salt
1 c. milk	1 tsp. parsley flakes
1/2 tsp. salt	2 bay leaves
1/4 tsp. pepper	1 pt. oysters

Combine the cream and milk in a saucepan and season with the salt, pepper, celery salt, parsley flakes and bay leaves. Scald the milk mixture but do not boil. Add the oysters and simmer for 3 to 5 minutes or until edges begin to curl. Remove bay leaves and serve. 4-6 servings.

Mrs. Hatcher H. Ankers, Vienna, Virginia

GENERAL LEE'S VEGETABLE BOUILLON

4 c. chopped tomatoes	1 bay leaf
1 stalk celery, chopped	2 tsp. onion juice
2 carrots, chopped	Salt and pepper to taste
2 sprigs of parsley	1/2 c. sherry
1/4 green pepper, chopped	

Place the tomatoes in a saucepan, then add the vegetables, seasonings and 2 cups water. Bring to a boil and cook for 30 minutes. Strain, then add the sherry to the broth and serve hot in bouillon cups.

Mrs. W. Ludwell Harrison, Huntington, West Virginia

CHOWCHOW

8 lge. carrots	1 1/2 qt. vinegar
12 onions	6 c. sugar
12 lge. sweet red peppers	3 tbsp. celery seed
2 hot peppers	3 tbsp. mustard seed
2 lge. heads cabbage	1/2 tsp. red pepper (opt.)
3/4 c. salt	

Chop all the vegetables together finely, then add the salt. Let stand for 3 hours and drain well. Combine the vinegar and sugar in a large kettle and stir until the sugar dissolves. Add the seasonings and the vegetable mixture and simmer for 20 minutes. Bring to a boil and pack into hot sterilized jars, covering with the liquid, then seal.

Ruby Elam, West Liberty, Kentucky

ASHEVILLE SALAD

1 pkg. unflavored gelatin	Salt to taste
1 can tomato soup	1 3-oz. package cream cheese
5/8 c. milk	1/2 c. chopped celery
Dash of red pepper	1/2 c. chopped olives
Dash of Worcestershire sauce	1 tsp. minced onion

Soften the gelatin in 1/4 cup cold water. Combine the soup and 1/2 cup milk in a saucepan and heat through. Add gelatin and stir until dissolved. Add seasonings and chill until thickened. Soften the cream cheese with the remaining milk and beat until fluffy. Stir into gelatin mixture, then fold in remaining ingredients. Pour into a mold and chill until firm. 8 servings.

Mrs. Virginia D. Webb, Gordonsville, Virginia

CHICKEN SALAD TULIP CUPS

1/2 c. cornmeal	1 c. finely chopped celery
1 1/2 c. sifted flour	2 hard-cooked eggs, diced
2 tsp. salt	1/4 tsp. pepper
1/2 c. shortening	1 tbsp. grated onion
4 to 6 tbsp. cold water	1/2 c. mayonnaise
2 c. chopped cooked chicken	

Preheat oven to 450 degrees. Sift the cornmeal, flour and 1 teaspoon salt together into a bowl and cut in shortening until mixture resembles coarse crumbs. Add the water gradually, mixing with a fork until pastry holds together, and divide into 2 parts. Roll each part on a floured board to a 9-inch square and cut each square into 4 squares. Shape each square over bottom of a custard cup and pleat edges, leaving corners to give tulip effect. Prick with a fork and place on cookie sheet. Bake for 12 to 15 minutes. Cool for 10 minutes and remove from custard cups. Combine the chicken, celery and eggs. Mix remaining salt, pepper, onion and mayonnaise and stir into chicken mixture. Chill. Fill tulip cups. 8 servings.

Mrs. Jiles Vestal, Abingdon, Virginia

DUTCH DANDELION SALAD

1 lb. young, tender dandelion greens	1 tbsp. flour
4 thick slices bacon	2 tbsp. sugar
1/2 c. salad dressing	1/4 c. vinegar
1 egg, lightly beaten	1 c. water
1 tsp. salt	2 hard-cooked eggs, sliced

Wash the dandelion greens and roll in a cloth, then pat dry. Place in a salad bowl. Fry the bacon until crisp, then drain. Pour the drippings over the dandelion greens. Blend the salad dressing, egg, salt, flour, sugar, vinegar and 1/4 cup water together, then pour into the skillet. Bring to a boil and cook, stirring constantly, until thickened. Pour while hot over the dandelion greens and toss well. Crumble the bacon over top and toss lightly. Garnish with the egg slices and serve immediately. 6 servings.

Mrs. Doris Taylor, Chesapeake, Virginia

PORK AND SWEET RELISH

2 c. diced cooked pork	1 tbsp. lemon juice
2 c. diced unpeeled red apples	1/4 tsp. onion juice
1 c. diced celery	Dash of salt
1/4 c. India or sweet relish	1/3 c. mayonnaise

Combine all the ingredients and mix well. Refrigerate until well chilled. Serve on lettuce. 4 servings.

Mrs. W. C. Dobbs, Arlington, Virginia

BAKED APPLES WITH SAUSAGE

6 lge. tart apples	1 tsp. salt
1 c. bulk sausage	2 tbsp. brown sugar

Wash the apples and cut slice from top. Remove cores and scoop out pulp, leaving shells 3/4 inch thick. Chop the pulp and combine with sausage, salt and brown sugar. Mix well. Fill the apples with sausage mixture and place in a baking pan. Bake at 375 degrees until done.

Mrs. Janice Cabler, Nashville, Tennessee

ROAST BEEF AND YORKSHIRE PUDDING

1 5-lb. standing rib roast	2 eggs
Salt and pepper	1 c. milk
1 c. sifted flour	

Rub the roast with salt and pepper to taste, then place on a rack in a baking pan. Bake at 450 degrees for 25 minutes. Reduce oven temperature to 300 degrees and bake for 16 to 18 minutes per pound longer. Sift the flour with 1/2 teaspoon salt, then stir in the eggs and milk. Beat until smooth, then refrigerate the batter for at least 1 hour. Remove the roast from the oven. Increase oven temperature to 450 degrees. Spoon 3 tablespoons beef drippings into a 12 x 8-inch pan and heat pan in oven until drippings are smoking. Pour in the batter. Bake for 15 minutes or until puffy and browned. Cut in squares and serve immediately. 6 servings.

Loyce Cartwright, Dickinson, Texas

Festive Crown Roast and Potatoes with Pickle Sauce (below)

FESTIVE CROWN ROAST AND POTATOES WITH PICKLE SAUCE

1 7-lb. crown roast of pork	1/4 c. chopped dill pickle
Salt and coarsely ground pepper	3 tbsp. chopped parsley
3/4 c. dill pickle liquid	1/4 tsp. thyme leaves
1/3 c. chopped onion	1/4 tsp. tarragon leaves
1 tbsp. butter or margarine	2 tbsp. honey
1 16-oz. can tomatoes in puree	2 tbsp. sugar
1 env. brown gravy mix	1 1/2 tbsp. Dijon mustard
	3/4 c. water
	Seasoned Mashed Potatoes

Sprinkle the pork with salt and pepper, then place on rack in large shallow roasting pan. Roast in a 325 degree oven for 30 minutes per pound or until meat thermometer registers 170 degrees, brushing occasionally with 1/2 cup of the pickle liquid. Saute the onion in butter until golden in a saucepan, then add the tomatoes, gravy mix, chopped pickle, remaining pickle liquid, herbs, honey, sugar, mustard and water. Stir until blended, then cover and cook over low heat for 30 minutes, stirring occasionally. Pipe or spoon Seasoned Mashed Potatoes in center of pork roast about 20 minutes before end of roasting time. Place the roast on a platter. Garnish with pickles, then serve with the pickle sauce.

Seasoned Mashed Potatoes

3 lb. peeled potatoes, cubed	1/3 c. minced onion
1/2 c. milk	1/4 c. butter

1 pimento, minced   Salt to taste
1/4 minced parsley

Cook the potatoes in boiling water until tender, then drain, reserving 1/4 cup liquid. Mash the potatoes with the reserved liquid and milk. Saute the onion in the butter until tender. Add to potatoes with the pimento, parsley and salt.

ENGLISH BEEF PIE

1 2-lb. round steak	1/8 tsp. pepper
3 tbsp. flour	1 tsp. Worcestershire sauce
3 tbsp. fat	2 c. canned tomatoes
2 onions, sliced	1 1/2 c. sliced carrots
2 c. boiling water	3 c. sliced potatoes
2 tsp. salt	1 recipe biscuit dough

Cut the steak in 1-inch cubes and dredge with flour. Brown in fat in a skillet. Add onions and cook until soft. Add the water and cover. Simmer for 30 minutes or until steak is almost done. Add remaining ingredients except biscuit dough and cover. Simmer until vegetables are done, then place steak and vegetables in a greased 2-quart casserole. Thicken stock with additional flour blended with water and pour over steak mixture. Roll out biscuit dough to fit casserole and place over steak mixture. Bake at 425 degrees for 20 to 25 minutes. 6 servings.

Mrs. Currole McConnell, Montgomery, Alabama

SPICED BEEF WITH DUMPLINGS

1 4-lb. beef pot roast	1 tsp. salt
1 1-lb. can tomatoes	1/4 tsp. pepper
1/4 c. wine vinegar	1 pkg. refrigerator biscuits
1 clove of garlic, minced	1 tbsp. snipped parsley
6 whole cloves	2 tbsp. flour
1/2 tsp. mixed pickling spice	

Trim the excess fat from the roast, then melt the fat in a Dutch oven. Brown the roast on all sides in the hot fat. Add 1/4 cup water and the remaining ingredients except the biscuits, parsley and flour. Cover and simmer for 2 hours and 30 minutes or until tender. Place the biscuits on the roast and sprinkle with the parsley. Cover tightly and steam for 15 minutes or till dumplings are done. Remove the roast and dumplings to a warm platter. Combine the flour and 1/4 cup water and stir into the pan juices. Cook, stirring, until thickened. Serve with the roast.

Mrs. Betty Peters, Bassett, Virginia

MOUNTAIN-STYLE RABBIT

1 dressed rabbit, disjointed	1 c. onions, chopped
Vinegar	1/2 lb. prunes
4 slices salt pork	3 bay leaves
1 tbsp. butter	1/4 tsp. pepper

Marinate the rabbit overnight in equal amounts of vinegar and water to cover. Drain. Brown the salt pork in a heavy pot, then add the butter and melt. Add the rabbit and brown well. Add onions, prunes and seasonings. Cover with boiling water. Cook slowly, covered, for 1 hour and 30 minutes or until rabbit is tender.

Mrs. Francine Quertinmont, Buckhannon, West Virginia

VENISON ROAST

1 6-lb. leg roast	2 peppercorns
1 fifth red cooking wine	1 clove of garlic, crushed
2 tsp. mustard seed	1 tsp. salt
2 bay leaves	2 c. water
Pinch of thyme	1/8 lb. salt pork

Remove all the fat from the roast and wipe with a damp cloth. Mix the remaining ingredients except the salt pork in large crock or roaster, then place the roast in marinade mixture. Refrigerate for at least 24 hours, turning occasionally. Remove the roast from the marinade and lard generously with the salt pork. Place in a baking pan. Bake in 475-degree oven for about 15 minutes. Reduce the oven temperature to 325 degrees and bake for 25 minutes per pound longer, basting frequently with the marinade. Thicken the pan juices for gravy and add 1 cup sour cream before serving, if desired. 12 servings.

Mrs. Fred H. Arnold, Richmond, Virginia

HAM-DRIED APPLES AND KNEPPEN

2 c. dried apples	1/2 tsp. salt
1 1 1/2-lb. ham	1 egg, beaten
2 tbsp. brown sugar	2 tbsp. melted butter
2 c. flour	Milk
3 1/2 tsp. baking powder	

Cover the apples with water and soak overnight. Place the ham in a kettle and cover with cold water. Cover and simmer for 3 hours. Add the apples and brown sugar, and cook for 1 hour longer. Combine the flour, baking powder and salt in a bowl, then add the egg and butter. Stir in enough milk to make a stiff dough. Drop dough by spoonfuls into the boiling ham and apples. Cover pan tightly and cook for 10 to 12 minutes. Do not lift cover until ready to serve.

Laura F. Willcox, South Norfolk, Virginia

OLD VIRGINIA COUNTRY-FRIED HAM WITH RED-EYE GRAVY

1 lge. center cut ham slice,	1/8 tsp. salt
1/2 in. thick	1/2 c. strong hot coffee

Slash the fat on edge of ham in several places. Place the ham in a hot skillet and brown on one side over high heat. Turn and brown lightly on other side. Cover and cook over low heat for 15 minutes or until tender. Remove from the skillet and place on a heated platter. Sprinkle salt in the skillet and add the coffee. Boil for 2 minutes, then pour over the ham. Serve with biscuits. 4 servings.

Mrs. Martha Henegar, Jellico, Tennessee

SMITHFIELD HAM

1 Smithfield ham	1 c. (packed) brown sugar
2 c. vinegar	1/2 c. flour
2 c. dark syrup	1 tbsp. prepared mustard

Scrub the ham well. Place the ham in a roaster and cover with cold water. Soak overnight, then drain and rinse. Return ham to roaster, then combine the vinegar and syrup and pour over the ham. Add enough water to cover. Bring to a boil, then simmer for about 4 hours. Remove the ham from the roaster and remove the skin immediately. Trim off excess fat and cool. Combine the brown sugar, flour, mustard and enough water to make a smooth paste. Spread over ham. Place ham in baking pan. Bake at 350 degrees until heated through.

Mrs. Vivian Snell, Norfolk, Virginia

SADDLE OF LAMB WITH STUFFING

Saddle of young lamb	1 tbsp. butter
1 onion or garlic clove, halved	1 c. bread crumbs
Salt and pepper to taste	2 eggs, well beaten
1/2 lb. lean ham	2 tbsp. flour
1 tsp. chopped parsley	1 c. beef stock
6 shallots, chopped	

Remove the bones and as much fat as possible from the saddle of lamb and rub all over with the onion, salt and pepper. Place in a baking pan and refrigerate overnight. Chop the ham fine and add parsley and shallots. Cook in the butter in a saucepan until golden and season with salt and pepper. Add the bread crumbs and eggs and mix well. Stuff the saddle with ham mixture, roll and tie with string. Roast at 350 degrees for 1 hour to 1 hour and 30 minutes, basting frequently. Pour off all except 2 tablespoons pan drippings and stir in flour until smooth. Add the beef stock gradually and cook, stirring constantly, until thickened. Serve with the lamb.

Mrs. Kenneth Underwood, Montgomery, Alabama

LIBERTY CHICKEN

2 chickens, quartered	1 tsp. oregano
1 c. salad oil	1 clove of garlic, minced
1/3 c. lemon juice	1 tsp. salt
3 tbsp. soy sauce	1/4 tsp. pepper

Place chickens in a flat pan. Combine the remaining ingredients and pour over the chickens. Marinate for 4 to 5 hours, turning occasionally. Cook chickens over charcoal fire slowly for 1 hour and 30 minutes, turning frequently and brushing with the marinade. 8 servings.

Mrs. Arlon W. Johnson, Danville, Virginia

VIRGINIA-STYLE FRIED CHICKEN

1 lge. fryer	Pepper
Flour	1 c. white cornmeal
Salt	2 c. milk

Cut the chicken in serving pieces. Mix 3/4 cup flour and salt and pepper to taste in a paper bag. Add the chicken and shake until coated. Fry in bacon fat in a skillet until golden brown on both sides. Remove from skillet. Drain fat from skillet and reserve. Place chicken in skillet and add 3/4 cup water. Cover and cook over low heat until tender. Remove cover and cook until crisp. Remove from skillet and keep warm. Mix the cornmeal and 1 teaspoon salt in a saucepan. Stir in 2 cups boiling water and cook over medium heat, stirring constantly, until thick. Drop by large spoonfuls into small amount of reserved fat in the skillet and cook until brown on both sides. Keep warm. Heat 3 tablespoons reserved fat in the skillet and stir in 3 tablespoons flour. Cook until dark brown, stirring constantly. Add the milk and cook over low heat, stirring, until thickened. Add salt and pepper to taste. Serve chicken on a large platter and surround with fried mush. Spoon cream gravy over the fried mush just before serving.

Mrs. E. O. Willis, Jr., Culpeper, Virginia

WAFFLES WITH CHICKEN LIVERS

2 c. white cornmeal	1 1/2 tsp. salt
1 1/2 c. boiling water	2 eggs, separated
3 c. flour	1 1/2 c. milk
3 tbsp. sugar	4 tbsp. melted shortening
4 tsp. baking powder	

Mix the cornmeal and water in a saucepan and cook over low heat for 20 minutes, stirring frequently. Sift remaining dry ingredients together and stir into the cornmeal mixture. Add egg yolks, milk and shortening and mix well. Beat the egg whites until stiff and fold into cornmeal mixture. Bake in hot waffle iron.

Sauteed Chicken Livers

1 lb. chicken livers, halved	1 can onion soup
Flour	1 sm. can mushroom pieces

Heat small amount of fat in large skillet. Dredge the chicken livers with flour and brown in fat in the skillet. Add onion soup and mushrooms and simmer for 20 to 30 minutes. Serve on waffles.

Mrs. R. L. Anderson, Travelers Rest, South Carolina

STUFFED DUCKLINGS WITH BRUSSELS SPROUTS

2 6-oz. packages long grain and wild rice mix	1 lb. small white onions
1/4 c. butter or margarine	3 pkg. frozen California Brussels sprouts
1 c. chopped onion	1/4 c. flour
2 c. diced celery	2 c. chicken broth
2 5-lb. ducklings	3 tbsp. chopped fresh parsley

Combine the rice mix, butter, 4 cups water, onion and celery in a large saucepan and bring to a boil. Reduce the heat and cover, then cook slowly for 20 minutes or until the rice is tender. Stuff the ducklings with the rice mixture and close body cavities with skewers. Place the ducklings, breast side up, on a rack in large shallow roasting pan. Roast at 400 degrees for 15 minutes, then reduce the oven temperature to 325 degrees and roast for 2 hours longer or until ducklings test done. Cook the onions in boiling salted water for 15 minutes or until tender, then drain. Cook the Brussels sprouts according to package directions, then drain and combine with the onions. Keep warm. Place the ducklings on a serving platter, then add 2 tablespoons of the drippings to the Brussels sprouts and onions. Pour 1/4 cup of the drippings into a saucepan and blend in the flour. Stir in the chicken broth and parsley. Cook, stirring, until the sauce boils for 1 minute. Pour half the sauce over the vegetables and serve the remaining sauce with the ducklings.

Stuffed Ducklings with Brussels Sprouts (above)

HERB-FRIED QUAIL

1/2 c. flour	1/8 tsp. pepper
1 tsp. salt	8 quail
1 tsp. paprika	1/2 c. buttermilk
1/2 tsp. dried thyme leaves	Salad oil or shortening

Mix the flour and seasonings together in a bowl. Dip the quail into the buttermilk, then roll in the seasoned flour. Heat 1/4 inch oil in heavy skillet until drop of water sizzles when added. Fry the quail for about 15 minutes on each side or until browned. Drain on paper towels. Serve. Yield: 2-4 servings.

Linda Adamson, Danville, Virginia

TURKEY AND CORN BREAD DRESSING

1 1/2 c. finely chopped onion	1/8 tsp. pepper
1 1/2 c. finely chopped celery	1/2 tsp. poultry seasoning
1/3 c. butter	1/2 tsp. sage
8 c. crumbled corn bread	1 egg, well beaten
1 1/2 tsp. salt	1 12-lb. turkey, cooked

Cook the onion and celery in butter in a large saucepan until tender. Add the corn bread and sprinkle with seasonings. Add the egg and mix. Add enough boiling water to moisten and mix well. Place in a casserole. Bake at 400 degrees until brown. Slice the turkey and serve with dressing.

Joyce Henson, Yazoo City, Mississippi

GARLIC-BROILED LOBSTER-TAILS

1 pkg. frozen lobster-tails	1 tsp. monosodium glutamate (opt.)
1 stick butter, melted	1 tsp. garlic salt
1 tsp. salt	2 tbsp. lemon juice

Drop the lobster-tails into boiling salted water and cook for 10 minutes, then remove from water and cool. Combine the remaining ingredients in a small saucepan and keep warm. Trim the shell and loosen the lobster meat from shell. Place in a shallow pan and baste with the butter mixture. Broil until brown, basting frequently. Serve immediately.

Mrs. Sue Compton, Dozier, Alabama

SHRIMP CARDINALE

3 sm. onions, chopped	1 tbsp. lemon juice
1/4 lb. butter or margarine	1/2 c. catsup
1 1/2-lb. large shelled	1 tsp. salt
shrimp, deveined	Pepper to taste
1/2 lb. fresh mushrooms,	1 c. grated Cheddar cheese
sliced	1/4 c. cream
3 tbsp. paprika	1/2 stick softened butter
1/4 c. white wine	1/3 c. flour
2 tbsp. sherry	Whipped hot potatoes

Saute the onions in the butter until golden, then add the shrimp and stir until slightly pink. Simmer for 2 minutes. Stir in the mushrooms and saute lightly. Sprinkle the paprika over the shrimp mixture and stir. Add the wines, lemon juice, catsup, salt, pepper and half the cheese. Simmer for 5 minutes, then stir in the cream. Combine the butter and flour to form a ball, then add and stir until thickened, adding water if needed. Place the potatoes in a 12 x 7 x 2-inch baking dish and shape around edges to make a nest, then pour in the shrimp mixture. Sprinkle the remaining cheese over the top. Bake at 400 degrees until cheese is melted and lightly browned. 8 servings.

Mrs. R. L. Slawson, Alexandria, Virginia

SEAFOOD BRUNCH SPECIAL

1/2 lb. cleaned cooked shrimp, deveined	Pinch of curry powder
1/2 lb. crab meat	3 c. cooked rice
1 c. hot med. white sauce	1/2 c. shredded Cheddar cheese
1/2 c. cooked peas	2 tsp. prepared mustard
1/4 c. halved pimento-stuffed olives	1 egg, slightly beaten
1/8 tsp. hot sauce	1/2 c. dry bread crumbs
	2 tbsp. melted butter
	1/8 tsp. salt

Add the shrimp and crab meat to the white sauce, then stir in the peas, olives and seasonings. Simmer until heated through. Combine the rice, cheese, mustard and egg and form into 6 firm balls. Combine the crumbs, butter and salt in a pie pan and roll the rice balls in the crumb mixture, turning to coat. Place on a buttered cookie sheet, then flatten slightly and press into nests. Bake at 350 degrees for 15 minutes or until firm and lightly browned. Fill the nests with hot seafood mixture. 6 servings.

Seafood Brunch Special (above)

EDGEWATER SHAD ROE AMANDINE

1 pair shad roe	1 1/2 tsp. butter
2 c. bouillon	1/2 c. toasted slivered
2 tbsp. lemon juice	almonds
4 strips bacon	

Drop the roe into the boiling bouillon, then add the lemon juice and simmer for 5 minutes. Pour off the bouillon and rinse the roe in cold water. Remove the center vein carefully. Fry the bacon until crisp in a skillet, then drain on paper towels. Drain off all the drippings from skillet except 2 tablespoons. Add the butter and the roe and saute for about 15 minutes, turning to brown on all sides. Remove to a hot platter. Add the almonds to the skillet and stir over high heat until browned, then pour almonds over the roe. Serve with the bacon and lemon wedges.

Mrs. Jamie Madison, Hampton, Virginia

STUFFED ROCKFISH

4 1-lb. rockfish	1/2 tsp. thyme
3 tsp. salt	3 drops of hot sauce
2 tbsp. cooking oil	1 pkg. onion soup mix
4 c. buttered bread crumbs	1 tsp. Worcestershire sauce

Cover the rockfish with water, then sprinkle with the salt. Soak for 20 minutes, then drain. Dry with paper towels. Rub inside and out with the oil. Combine the remaining ingredients and 3/4 cup hot water and mix well. Stuff the rockfish with the crumb mixture, then place on foil and seal. Place in a shallow pan. Bake at 350 degrees for 1 hour. Open foil and baste rockfish with drippings. Increase oven temperature to 450 degrees and bake until browned. Garnish with lemon slices.

Mrs. Hazel S. Courtney, Hartwood, Virginia

GERMAN OYSTER POTPIE

1 c. shortening	2 pt. oysters
3 c. flour	Salt and pepper to taste
1/2 lb. butter	

Cut the shortening into the flour until crumbly, then add enough water to hold dough together. Divide the dough into 3 parts. Roll out 1 part thin and place in Dutch oven to cover bottom and halfway up side. Dot with half the butter, then add half the oysters and season with salt and pepper. Roll out another part of the dough and cover the oysters. Dot with the remaining butter, then add the remaining oysters and sprinkle with salt and pepper. Roll out the remaining dough and place over the oysters. Cut steam vents in dough. Bake at 375 degrees for 1 hour. Let stand 10 minutes before serving. 8 servings.

Barbara Jean Groves, Summersville, West Virginia

BUBBLE AND SQUEAK

1 5-lb. corned beef brisket	6 whole white onions
1 med. onion, halved	4 pkg. frozen California
1 clove of garlic	Brussels sprouts
6 whole cloves	1 16-oz. can whole baby
8 peppercorns	carrots, drained
2 bay leaves	2 tbsp. snipped parsley
1 c. sliced celery	English Mustard Sauce
6 med. potatoes, peeled	

Place the corned beef in a large pot and cover with cold water. Add the halved onion, seasonings and celery. Bring to a boil, then reduce the heat and cover. Simmer for 3 to 4 hours or until tender. Skim the excess fat from liquid and remove the corned beef. Cook the potatoes and whole onions, covered, in the corned beef liquid until almost tender. Add the Brussels sprouts and cover, then cook for 15 minutes longer. Add the carrots and heat through. Serve the beef and vegetables on hot platters. Garnish the potatoes with parsley. Serve with English Mustard Sauce.

English Mustard Sauce

1 tbsp. cornstarch	1 tbsp. butter
2 tsp. sugar	1/4 c. vinegar
1 tsp. dry mustard	1 tsp. horseradish
1/2 tsp. salt	2 beaten egg yolks

Combine the cornstarch, sugar, dry mustard and salt in top of a double boiler, then stir in 1 cup water. Cook and stir over direct low heat until mixture thickens and boils for 1 minute. Remove from heat and mix in the butter, vinegar and horseradish, then stir in the egg yolks. Cook, stirring constantly, over boiling water until sauce thickens slightly.

Bubble and Squeak (above)

BEETS WITH ORANGE SAUCE

1/2 c. sugar	1/4 c. orange juice
2 tsp. cornstarch	1 tbsp. butter
1 tsp. grated orange rind	1 No. 303 can beets, drained
1 tbsp. lemon juice	

Combine the sugar and the cornstarch in a saucepan, then stir in 1/2 cup boiling water. Cook for 5 minutes, stirring constantly. Add the orange rind, lemon juice, orange juice and butter and heat through. Pour over the hot beets. 5 servings.

Mrs. Shirley Flynn, Hot Springs, Virginia

FRIED GREEN TOMATOES

4 med. tomatoes	Flour
Salt and pepper to taste	Shortening

Slice the tomatoes in 1/2-inch slices, then sprinkle with salt and pepper. Dredge with flour. Brown on both sides in hot shortening in heavy skillet. 4 servings.

Mrs. Esther Geer, Falls Church, Virginia

FRIED SQUASH

4 med. squash	1/2 c. shortening
1 c. cornmeal	

Wash and slice the squash, then soak in salted water for 10 to 15 minutes. Dip into cornmeal, then fry in hot shortening until golden brown on both sides.

Lena E. Wyatt, Gretna, Virginia

GREEN LIMAS A LA CREME

2 c. shelled green limas	1/3 c. light cream
1/4 c. grated Cheddar cheese	Salt and pepper to taste
1 tbsp. butter or margarine	

Cook the limas in a saucepan in salted water until tender, then drain. Add the remaining ingredients and heat thoroughly, stirring frequently until the cheese is melted. 4 servings.

Mrs. Charles W. Cooke, Galax, Virginia

SPICY RED CABBAGE WITH APPLES

1 qt. shredded red cabbage	1/3 c. sugar
2 peeled tart apples, sliced	4 whole cloves
1/4 c. red wine vinegar	3 tbsp. butter or margarine
1 1/4 tsp. salt	1/2 c. water

Combine all the ingredients in medium saucepan. Cook, covered, over medium heat for about 25 minutes or until cabbage is tender, stirring occasionally. 4-6 servings.

Mrs. Page Inman, Portsmouth, Virginia

VIRGINIA-STYLE SWEET POTATOES

4 sm. sweet potatoes, peeled	1/2 stick butter
1 1/2 c. sugar	Milk

Grate the sweet potatoes and place in a buttered casserole. Sprinkle the sugar over the potatoes, then cut the butter over sugar. Add milk to just below top of potatoes but do not mix or stir. Bake at 300 degrees for 1 hour and 30 minutes. 8 servings.

Mrs. Leroy Gillie, Bluefield, West Virginia

OLIEBOLLEN

1 c. milk	3 c. flour
1 tbsp. sugar	1 1/3 c. chopped apple
1/2 tsp. salt	1/2 c. currants
2 tbsp. margarine	1/4 c. chopped candied orange
1 pkg. yeast	peel
1 egg	

Scald the milk, then stir in the sugar, salt and margarine. Cool to lukewarm. Place 1/4 cup warm water into a large warm bowl, then sprinkle in the yeast and stir until dissolved. Add the milk mixture, egg, half the flour, apple, currants and orange peel, then beat until smooth. Mix in the remaining flour. Cover and let rise in warm place, free from draft, for about 1 hour or until doubled in bulk. Beat the batter down. Drop by small teaspoonfuls into deep fat at 375 degrees and fry until golden brown, then drain. Sprinkle with confectioners' sugar, if desired. Serve warm.

Oliebollen (above)

POPOVERS

2 eggs

1 c. milk

1 c. sifted all-purpose flour

1/4 tsp. salt

Beat the eggs slightly in a bowl, then add the milk. Add the flour and salt and beat vigorously for 2 minutes. Pour the batter into hot greased custard cups or small individual loaf pans, filling 2/3 full. Bake at 425 degrees for about 40 minutes. 6 large popovers.

Sharon Schieman, Fairmont, West Virginia

SALLY LUNN

1 pkg. yeast

1/4 c. warm water

2 c. scalded milk

2/3 c. shortening

2 tsp. salt

1/4 c. sugar

3 eggs, beaten

6 c. flour

Sprinkle the yeast over the water, then stir to dissolve. Combine the milk, shortening, salt and sugar in a mixing bowl, and cool to lukewarm. Add the yeast and eggs and beat until smooth. Add the flour gradually, beating well after each addition. Let rise until doubled in bulk, then punch down. Turn into 1 large greased pan and let rise until doubled in bulk. Bake in 350-degree oven for about 1 hour.

Mrs. H. E. Doss, Covington, Virginia

SOUTHERN SPOON BREAD

2 c. milk

1 c. white cornmeal

1 tbsp. sugar

1 tsp. salt

2 tbsp. butter

4 eggs, separated

Scald the milk, then stir in cornmeal gradually. Cook in a double boiler, stirring constantly, until thick. Mix in the sugar, salt and butter. Remove from heat and cool slightly. Stir in beaten egg yolks, then fold in the stiffly beaten egg whites. Pour into a well-buttered 2-quart casserole. Bake at 350 degrees for about 45 minutes. 8 servings.

Mrs. W. O. Pinson, Richmond, Virginia

GERMAN SOUR CREAM TWISTS

3 1/2 c. sifted flour

1 tsp. salt

1 c. shortening

1 pkg. dry yeast

1/4 c. warm water

3/4 c. sour cream

1 egg

2 egg yolks

1 tsp. vanilla

1 c. sugar

Sift the flour and salt into a mixing bowl and cut in shortening. Dissolve the yeast in water and stir into flour mixture. Stir in the sour cream, egg, egg yolks and vanilla until well mixed. Cover with a damp cloth and refrigerate for 2 hours. Roll out half the dough at a time on a sugared board to an 8 x 16-inch rectangle. Fold ends toward center with ends overlapping. Sprinkle with sugar and roll out again to same size. Repeat a third time. Cut into 1 x 4-inch strips. Twist ends in opposite directions, stretching slightly, and place on ungreased baking sheet in shape of horseshoes. Bake at 375 degrees for 15 minutes. Remove from baking sheet immediately.

Mrs. Connie Carr, Nashville, Tennessee

LORD JIM'S MINCEMEAT PLUM PUDDING

4 c. drained mincemeat	1 1/2 c. (packed) dark brown
3 c. coarse dry bread crumbs	sugar
1 tbsp. cinnamon	6 eggs
1 1/2 tsp. ginger	5/8 c. brandy
1/2 tsp. nutmeg	6 tbsp. red wine
1/4 tsp. salt	1/4 c. milk

Combine the mincemeat, bread crumbs, spices, salt and brown sugar in a large mixing bowl. Beat the eggs until foamy, then add 6 tablespoons brandy, red wine and milk. Stir the egg mixture into the mincemeat mixture with a wooden spoon, mixing well. Spoon into a buttered 2-quart pudding mold and cover with lid. Place the mold on a rack in large pot, then fill the pot half way up the side of mold with boiling water. Cover pot and steam for 4 hours, checking water level occasionally and adding water if needed. Let pudding cool slightly before turning out of mold. Soak a cheesecloth in the remaining brandy and wrap the pudding to store. Return to mold and steam for 1 hour and 30 minutes before serving. Drizzle with confectioners' icing and serve with hard sauce, if desired.

Lord Jim's Mincemeat Plum Pudding (above)

Apple Pudding (below)

APPLE PUDDING

2 qt. peeled apple slices	1/2 c. diet margarine
1 1/2 c. flour	1 c. sugar
1 tbsp. baking powder	1 egg
1/2 tsp. salt	1/2 tsp. cinnamon

Arrange the apples in a 2-quart glass baking dish. Sift the flour, baking powder and salt together. Cream the margarine, then add 3/4 cup sugar gradually, beating well. Beat in the egg. Add the flour mixture alternately with 3/4 cup water and beat until smooth. Pour the batter over the apples. Blend the remaining sugar and cinnamon together and sprinkle over the batter. Bake at 375 degrees for 45 minutes or pudding tests done. Serve warm. 8 servings.

WILLIAMSBURG ORANGE-WINE CAKE

Rind of 1 med. orange	1/2 c. chopped nuts
1 c. raisins	2 c. flour
1/2 c. butter or shortening	1 tsp. soda
1 c. sugar	1/2 tsp. salt
2 eggs, beaten	1 c. milk or sour milk
1 tsp. vanilla	

Grind orange rind and raisins. Cream butter and sugar until light. Add eggs, vanilla, nuts, raisins and rind. Sift flour with soda and salt, then add alternately with milk. Pour into a greased 9 x 13-inch pan or 8-inch square pan. Bake for 30 to 40 minutes at 350 degrees or until done. Frost or glaze.

Wine Icing

1/3 c. butter	1 tbsp. grated orange rind (opt.)
2 c. confectioners' sugar	Sherry

Mix all ingredients, adding enough sherry to make a spreading consistency. Spread on cooled cake.

Glaze

Juice of 1 orange	1/2 c. sugar

Combine juice and sugar; bring to a boil. Pour over warm cake. Yield: 16 servings.

Mrs. William J. Wheeler, Norfolk, Virginia

HARVEST SWEET POTATO PIE

1 3/4 c. mashed sweet potatoes	1 c. sugar
1 tsp. salt	1 tsp. cinnamon
1 1/2 c. milk	1 unbaked pie shell
2 eggs, slightly beaten	

Combine all the filling ingredients in a bowl, then beat until smooth. Pour into the pie shell. Bake at 350 degrees for 30 minutes or until knife inserted near the center comes out clean.

Mrs. Shirley Wise, Richmond, Virginia

TIPSY PARSON

1 10-oz. sponge cake	Dash of salt
1 lb. blanched slivered almonds	4 c. milk, scalded
1 1/4 c. sherry	6 egg yolks, slightly beaten
3/4 c. sugar	1 tsp. vanilla
1/2 c. sifted flour	2 c. heavy cream

Slice the cake and line side and bottom of a large bowl, then sprinkle with the almonds. Spoon 1 cup sherry over all the cake. Combine 1/2 cup sugar, flour and salt in a large saucepan, then stir in the milk gradually. Cook, stirring constantly, for 2 minutes or until thickened. Cool. Stir the cooled milk mixture into the egg yolks gradually, then, cook, stirring constantly, for 5 minutes. Cool thoroughly, then stir in the vanilla. Pour over the cake carefully. Whip the cream until stiff peaks form, adding the remaining sugar and the remaining sherry gradually. Spread over the pudding, then chill for several hours.

Mrs. Ophelia Owens, Richmond, Virginia

favorite
foods of
the carolinas

Like the Virginias, the Carolinas represent opposite ends of a cultural spectrum. At one end there is South Carolina with its plantations once so rich that the entire region was referred to as the four kingdoms: tobacco, indigo, rice, and sugar. The foods that appear on the tables in this part of the Deep South make extensive use of rice in such dishes as Sausage-Peanut Pilau and Crab and Wild Rice. There is a distinctive French accent in the cookery, too, brought by the many French Huguenots who settled in and around Charleston. This accent is apparent in recipes like Brioche with Rum Fruit.

At the other end of the spectrum lies North Carolina, a land of small farms and mountain communities. This part of the Deep South provided many of the pioneers who, after moving down from western Virginia, moved again and began to populate western Georgia, Alabama, Mississippi, and Louisiana. Their foods were simpler than those of South Carolina and featured Fried Squirrel, Rebel Yell Fried Grits, and other simple dishes

The section that follows contains home-tested, time-proven recipes from both parts of the Carolinas. They form a montage against which it is possible to measure all the influences that have gone into developing the region's cuisine. They are recipes you'll come to depend upon when you want to serve authentic Deep South recipes with a touch of the Carolinas in them.

One of the most romantic of all American mysteries centers around a tiny, sheltered island off the North Carolina coast. Here, on Roanoke Island in the year 1587, Sir Walter Raleigh established what he hoped would be the first permanent British colony in North America. After assisting the more than 100 settlers in erecting a palisade or fort and sowing their fields, he went home to England promising to send back needed supplies and more colonists. But England was more concerned over the threat of the Spanish Armada than with colonizing the New World. Three years passed before a ship returned to Roanoke Island. Its crew found the settlers gone, the palisade full of high grass, and tools and weapons lying on the ground, rusting. Only the enigmatic word "Croatoan" carved on a tree gave any clue to what might have

HISTORY AND TRADITIONS OF
the carolinas

happened. To this day, legends abound throughout the Carolinas as to what befell the mysterious "Lost Colony."

SOUTH CAROLINA

Nearly a hundred years later, in 1670, another expedition set out from England for the Carolinas. This one was not nearly so tragic in its ending: it formed the beginning of South Carolina. Charles II had granted Lord Anthony Ashley and Sir John Colleton rights to all the land between Virginia and Spanish-dominated Florida. It was hoped this colony could grow the tropical commodities Virginia had failed to yield — indigo, silk, wine, currants, olives, and the like. After exploring the South Carolina coast, the colonists landed and built their settlement, Charles Town, between the Ashley and Cooper rivers.

The character of social life in the new colony was firmly established by the arrival in 1680 of a shipload of French Huguenots, Protestants seeking to enjoy the new colony's promised religious freedom. Thousands more of these refugees arrived in the years after 1685 when freedom of religion was abolished in France. They brought with them not only years of experience in wine producing, silkworm raising, and olive growing, but a lifestyle destined to leave a permanent imprint on South Carolina.

The new colonists established plantations along the marshy lowlands of the coast, plantations ideally suited for the growing of rice. They also helped build up one of the loveliest and most romantic of all southern cities, Charleston. The French Carolinians believed that while plantation life was enjoyable, even more enjoyable was the constant companionship of their fellow man. So they established in the New World one of the traditions of the Old — that of the town house. Virtually every plantation owner had his town house where he and his family lived during the social season, usually that time when the crops did not have to be planted or harvested.

The English settlers of South Carolina emulated their French neighbors, and soon a thriving cosmopolitan city evolved. An important part of the culture of that city were the elegant, leisurely meals served around great tables gleaming with much polish and reflected candlelight. Rice, a staple crop of the region, almost always appeared on the menu. And the talented African cooks who dominated many South Carolina kitchens made their contributions, too, such as the combination of rice with vegetables, meats, or seafood called "pilau," a dish that even today is characteristic of South Carolina.

NORTH CAROLINA

To the north and west of South Carolina lay North Carolina, a vastly different region. The contrast between the two Carolinas reminds one of the differences between the two Virginias. Here had settled many one-time indentured servants, together with strongly independent Scottish refugees from the Old World and Scots-Irish who had been forceably resettled from northern Ireland.

Their foods were those of the land they lived on: wild game birds and animals, fish, and those vegetables that could be grown in often inhospitable soil. Stews and cornbreads often appeared on their tables; simplicity was the theme of North Carolina meals as much as elegance dominated those of South Carolina.

CUCUMBER SOUP

2 lb. cucumbers	1 green pepper,
Salt and pepper to taste	chopped (opt.)
1/2 c. hot water	1 tbsp. melted butter
1 med. onion, chopped	2 c. light cream
1 clove of garlic,	2 tbsp. chopped parsley
pressed (opt.)	

Peel and chop the cucumbers, then place in a large saucepan. Add the salt, pepper, water, onion, garlic and green pepper and cook until cucumbers are tender. Remove from heat and cool. Place in a blender container and blend until pureed. Stir in the butter and light cream. Serve hot or cold and garnish with the parsley. 6 servings.

Miss Isabel Dalmas, Valdese, North Carolina

SHE-CRAB SOUP

4 qt. water	1 1/2 tsp. finely grated onion
Salt	1 tsp. finely grated lemon
12 live 1/2-lb. blue she	peel
crabs	1/2 tsp. mace
4 tbsp. butter	1/2 tsp. white pepper
1 tbsp. flour	3 tbsp. dry sherry
2 c. milk	1 tbsp. finely chopped
2 c. heavy cream	parsley

Bring the water and 2 tablespoons salt to a boil in a 10-quart kettle. Drop the crabs in the water and bring to a boil. Reduce heat and cover tightly. Simmer for 15 minutes. Drain the crabs, then clean and remove crab meat. Set the crab meat and roe aside. Melt the butter in a heavy 4-quart saucepan, over moderate heat, then stir in the flour. Stir in the milk and cream slowly and cook, stirring constantly, until the mixture comes to a boil. Stir in the crab meat, crab roe, onion, lemon peel, mace, 1 1/2 teaspoons salt and white pepper. Reduce heat and simmer, partially covered, for 20 minutes. Stir in the sherry and pour into individual soup plates. Sprinkle with the parsley and serve at once. 4 servings.

Mrs. Elaine Atkins, Charleston, South Carolina

JELLIED ASPARAGUS SALAD

2 pkg. unflavored gelatin	1 sm. can asparagus tips,
3/4 c. sugar	drained
1/2 c. white vinegar	Juice of 1/2 lemon
1/2 tsp. salt	2 tsp. grated onion
2 pimentos, chopped	1 c. chopped celery

Soften the gelatin in 1/2 cup cold water. Mix the sugar, 1 cup water and vinegar in a saucepan and bring to a boil. Add the gelatin and stir until dissolved. Cool. Stir in remaining ingredients and pour into a mold. Chill until firm.

Dressing

1 c. sour cream	1/2 tsp. celery salt
1/4 c. lemon juice	1/2 tsp. paprika
2 tbsp. sugar	1 tsp. dry mustard
1 tsp. salt	1/4 tsp. garlic salt (opt.)
Cayenne pepper to taste	

Combine all ingredients in a bowl and blend with a rotary beater until smooth and thick. Serve with the salad.

Jimmie Garvin Harris, Aiken, South Carolina

HOPPING JOHN

1 ham hock, halved	1 tsp. salt
1 8-oz. package dried	1 tsp. cayenne pepper
black-eyed peas	1 c. rice
1 sm. onion, chopped	

Place the ham hock in a large saucepan and cover with water. Cook for 30 minutes. Add the peas, onion, salt, pepper and enough water to cover. Cook, covered, for 45 minutes, adding water as needed. Stir in the rice and cover. Cook for 30 minutes longer or until rice and peas are tender. May add 1 can tomatoes, if desired. 6 servings.

Hopping John (above)

BEEF WITH OKRA

1 lb. beef, cut in cubes	Salt and pepper to taste
2 pkg. frozen okra	Lemon juice to taste
1 sm. can tomato paste	1 c. long grain rice

Cook the beef in boiling, salted water until tender, then drain. Brown in small amount of fat in a skillet. Add 2 cups water, okra and tomato paste and cook until okra is done. Add the salt, pepper and lemon juice. Add 1 tablespoon fat to 2 cups boiling, salted water in a saucepan. Add the rice slowly, then boil for 10 minutes. Reduce heat and cook, without stirring, until all water evaporates. Serve the beef mixture over rice. 6 servings.

Irma Scott Hill, Cookeville, Tennessee

OVEN BEEF RAGOUT

1 1/2 lb. boneless beef	1/2 lb. mushroom caps
1 can beef consomme	1/4 lb. small white onions
3/4 c. water	1 tsp. salt
1/2 c. instant flour	1/8 tsp. pepper

Cut the beef into 1-inch cubes. Combine all ingredients in a 2 1/2-quart casserole and cover. Bake at 350 degrees for 30 minutes, then stir. Cover and bake for 2 hours to 2 hours and 30 minutes or until beef is tender.

Marilyn Clark, Council, North Carolina

HAM AND MACARONI CASSEROLE

1 7-oz. package elbow macaroni	1/2 tsp. salt
1/4 c. butter	1/8 tsp. pepper
1/2 c. chopped green pepper	1 1/2 c. milk
1/2 c. chopped celery	2 c. shredded Cheddar cheese
1/3 c. chopped onion	2 c. diced cooked ham
3 tbsp. flour	1 c. cottage cheese
2 tsp. celery seed	2 eggs, slightly beaten
	1/4 c. chopped pimento

Cook the macaroni according to package directions, then drain. Melt the butter in a 1-quart saucepan. Add the green pepper, celery and onion and cook over low heat for 2 to 3 minutes. Blend in the flour, celery seed, salt and pepper and remove from heat. Stir in the milk gradually, then cook over medium heat, stirring constantly, until mixture comes to a boil. Cook for 2 minutes, stirring frequently. Add the macaroni, Cheddar cheese, ham, cottage cheese, eggs and pimento and blend well. Turn into a buttered 2-quart casserole. Bake in 350-degree oven for 30 minutes. Remove from oven and let stand for several minutes. Garnish with parsley and serve. 8-10 servings.

Celia Stansbury, Asheville, North Carolina

Mince-Stuffed Baked Ham (below)

MINCE-STUFFED BAKED HAM

1 14-lb. fully cooked ham, boned	Currant jelly
Stuffing	Pistachio nuts, chopped

Preheat the oven to 325 degrees. Trim the rind off ham, leaving some around the shank. Fill hollow with stuffing, being careful not to pack too tightly. Remaining stuffing should be baked separately. Lace the opening together, using 5-inch skewers. Place the ham on a rack in a foil-lined roasting pan. Bake for 2 hours. Remove the ham from the oven and score the fat area. Spread currant jelly over scored area. Insert a meat thermometer into the center of the ham. Return the ham to the oven and bake for 30 minutes longer or until the thermometer reads 130 degrees. Remove the ham from oven and let stand for 10 minutes before carving. Sprinkle with pistachio nuts.

Stuffing

1/2 lb. pork sausage	2 c. whole blanched almonds
1/4 lb. butter	1 tsp. marjoram
1 c. diced onions	1 tsp. thyme
2 c. sliced celery	4 c. corn bread crumbs
2 c. mincemeat	2 c. dry bread crumbs

Brown sausage in a large frying pan, stirring and breaking up with a fork. Drain any excess fat from the sausage, then add the butter and melt. Saute the onions and celery in the sausage and butter for 5 minutes, then add the mincemeat and almonds and mix well. Stir in the marjoram and thyme. Remove from heat and place in a large mixing bowl. Add the corn bread and bread crumbs and mix lightly. Refrigerate until ready to stuff ham.

Roast Superb (below)

ROAST SUPERB

1 5-lb. rib eye beef roast	1/8 tsp. garlic powder
2 tsp. bon appetit	1/2 tsp. pepper
2 tsp. season-all	1/2 tsp. monosodium glutamate
1 tsp. dry mustard	1/2 tsp. salt
1 tsp. ginger	

Wipe the roast with a damp cloth. Combine the seasonings and rub thoroughly into roast. Place on a rack in pan, then insert a meat thermometer into the center of the thickest part. Roast in 325-degree oven for 2 hours for rare, or until meat thermometer registers desired degree of doneness. Serve on platter and garnish with parsley and radishes. 8-10 servings.

SUNDAY POT ROAST

1 4 to 5-lb. pot roast	1 c. chopped carrots
Cooking oil	1 c. chicken broth
1 c. chopped onions	1 c. cooking wine
1 c. chopped celery	

Cook the roast in a small amount of oil in a Dutch oven until brown. Remove roast from Dutch oven. Add the vegetables to the Dutch oven and cook until brown. Add the roast, broth, wine and enough water to cover roast, then cover the Dutch oven. Simmer for 2 to 3 hours, turning roast once. Remove roast to a warm platter. Thicken gravy, if desired, and serve with roast. 8 servings.

Mrs. James C. Hutto, Orangeburg, South Carolina

GERMAN-BOILED BEEF WITH EGG DUMPLINGS

1 5-lb. beef brisket	2 1/2 tsp. salt
6 carrots, sliced	2 eggs, separated
1 tsp. thyme	1 tbsp. milk
1 tbsp. chopped parsley	3 tbsp. flour
1 lge. onion, chopped	

Trim the brisket and cut into serving pieces. Place the brisket, carrots, thyme, parsley, onion and 2 teaspoons salt in a large kettle and add enough water to cover. Bring to a boil. Reduce heat and simmer for 1 hour and 30 minutes. Mix the egg yolks, milk and remaining salt in a bowl, then stir in the flour. Fold in stiffly beaten egg whites. Drop by spoonfuls onto beef mixture and cover. Cook for 15 minutes or until dumplings are done.

Mrs. Mildred Sherrer, Bay City, Texas

FRIED SQUIRREL

1 squirrel	1/2 c. flour
Salt	4 tbsp. shortening
1 med. onion, chopped	

Clean the squirrel and cut into serving pieces. Place in a container and cover with water. Add 1 tablespoon salt and soak for 2 hours or overnight. Drain. Place in a deep skillet with the onion and cover with water. Cook until tender. Drain the squirrel and reserve liquid. Mix the flour with 1/4 teaspoon salt and roll the squirrel in flour mixture. Fry in the shortening in a skillet until brown on all sides. Thicken the reserved liquid for gravy, if desired.

Mrs. E. G. Carter, Columbia, South Carolina

RAGOUT OF PORK WITH CHESTNUTS

6 tbsp. chopped pork fat	Red wine
6 lb. lean pork shoulder	4 c. canned whole chestnuts
Seasoned flour	2 tsp. sage
8 med. onions, thinly sliced	Chopped parsley
3 cloves of garlic, minced	

Place the pork fat in a Dutch oven and cook over medium heat until crisp, stirring frequently. Cut the pork shoulder into 1 1/2-inch cubes and dust with seasoned flour. Cook in pork fat over high heat, turning to brown evenly on all sides. Add the onions and garlic and cook for 2 minutes. Add enough wine to cover and bring to a boil. Cover. Bake at 350 degrees for 1 hour and 30 minutes to 2 hours. Drain the chestnuts and cut in half. Add to the pork mixture. Add the sage and more wine, if needed. Cover and bake for 30 to 35 minutes or until pork is tender. Garnish with the parsley and serve over rice. 8-10 servings.

Mrs. Horace Y. Kitchell, Greenwood, Mississippi

BARBECUED PORK TENDERLOIN

1 2 1/2-lb. pork tenderloin	1/2 tsp. paprika
1/2 c. flour	1/4 tsp. pepper
2 tbsp. shortening	2 tsp. celery seed
1/4 c. vinegar	2 tbsp. sugar
1/2 tsp. salt	1 tbsp. chili sauce
1/2 tsp. dry mustard	1/2 c. catsup

Cut the tenderloin into 8 slices and dredge with flour. Cook in the shortening in a skillet until brown. Combine remaining ingredients and pour over the pork. Cover. Bake at 350 degrees for 1 hour and 30 minutes, turning pork occasionally.

Mrs. Leon Sain, Lincolnton, North Carolina

STUFFED BUTTERFLY PORK CHOPS

1 c. finely chopped apple	1 1/2 tsp. salt
1/3 c. finely chopped celery	1 tsp. poultry seasoning
1/3 c. finely chopped onion	2 tbsp. meat stock
2 tbsp. butter or margarine	6 1-in. butterfly pork chops
3 c. dry bread cubes	with pockets
2 tbsp. raisins	1/8 tsp. pepper

Stuffed Butterfly Pork Chops (above)

Cook the apple, celery and onion in the butter until tender. Combine the bread cubes, raisins, 1/2 teaspoon salt, poultry seasoning and apple mixture, then add the meat stock, mixing thoroughly. Stuff each chop with the bread mixture. Brown chops in 2 tablespoons fat in a skillet, browning the unstuffed side first. Pour off the drippings. Season the chops with the remaining salt and pepper. Cover tightly and simmer for 45 minutes to 1 hour or until done adding a small amount of water if needed. Serve with green beans and onions. 6 servings.

STUFFED PORK CHOPS

4 pork chops, 2 in. thick	1/4 c. chopped celery
1 c. chopped apples	Salt and pepper to taste
1/4 c. chopped nuts	

Cut pockets in the pork chops. Combine remaining ingredients and stuff the pork chops. Secure openings. Brown in a skillet in small amount of fat, then cover. Bake at 350 degrees for 1 hour and 30 minutes.

Mrs. M. M. Person, Louisburg, North Carolina

SAUSAGE-PEANUT PILAF

1 lb. bulk pork sausage	1 can mushroom soup
1 c. finely sliced celery	1/4 c. chopped green pepper
1/2 c. chopped onion	1/3 c. chopped salted peanuts
1 c. cooked rice	8 stuffed green olives, sliced

Cook the sausage in a skillet until lightly browned. Add the celery and onion and cook for 3 minutes. Drain. Add rice, soup and green pepper and mix well. Pour into a 1-quart casserole and sprinkle with peanuts. Bake at 350 degrees for 30 minutes and top with olives. 4-6 servings.

Mrs. Carol Monroe, Greenville, South Carolina

CHICKEN CASSEROLE DELIGHT

3 chicken breasts	12 almonds
1 sm. can English peas, drained	1/2 c. corn flake crumbs
1 sm. can asparagus, drained	3 tbsp. melted butter
1/2 c. grated American cheese	

Cook the chicken breasts in boiling water until tender. Drain and reserve 1/2 cup broth. Bone the chicken and cut in small pieces. Place the English peas in a casserole and place chicken over peas. Add reserved broth. Add the asparagus and sprinkle with cheese. Add the almonds and crumbs and drizzle butter over top. Bake at 350 degrees for 25 to 30 minutes. 6 servings.

Mrs. Cecil A. McCall, Ellerbe, North Carolina

LEMON-BROILED CHICKEN

1 fryer, quartered	1/4 tsp. pepper
Juice of 2 lemons	1/2 tsp. paprika
1/2 c. melted butter	2 tbsp. sugar
2 tsp. salt	

Sprinkle the chicken with lemon juice and brush with butter. Place on rack in a broiler pan, skin side down. Combine remaining ingredients and sprinkle over chicken. Broil for 20 minutes, brushing with some of the remaining butter frequently. Turn and broil until brown and tender, brushing with remaining butter occasionally.

Mrs. Monroe Rogers, Marion, South Carolina

MISS MAGGIE'S CHICKEN PIE

1 recipe pastry for 2-crust pie	3/4 c. butter
1/2 c. flour	3 c. (about) chicken broth
3 c. chopped cooked chicken	Salt and pepper to taste

Line a 9-inch pie plate with pastry and sprinkle pastry with 1 tablespoon flour. Place chicken in pastry and dot with 6 tablespoons butter. Sprinkle 1 tablespoon flour over top. Pour in enough chicken broth to just cover chicken and sprinkle with salt and pepper. Place pastry on top of pie and cut slits in center of pastry. Seal edge. Bake at 425 degrees for 40 to 50 minutes or until brown. Melt remaining butter in a saucepan and stir in remaining flour. Cook over low heat, stirring, until smooth and brown. Add chicken and remaining broth and cook until thick, stirring occasionally. Season with salt and pepper and serve with pie.

Mrs. Guy F. Lane, Ramseur, North Carolina

OVEN-FRIED SESAME CHICKEN

2 broilers, halved	Cooking oil
1/2 tsp. ginger	Sesame seed
Salt and pepper to taste	

Sprinkle the chicken with ginger, salt and pepper and brush with oil. Pour oil to a depth of 1/8 inch in a 9 x 13-inch baking dish and place chicken, skin side down, in dish. Sprinkle with sesame seed. Bake at 400 degrees for 30 minutes. Turn and sprinkle with sesame seed. Bake for 30 minutes longer.

Mrs. Murray Steed, Brundidge, Alabama

PECAN-STUFFED CHICKEN BREASTS

4 sm. chicken breasts	1/2 c. chopped pecans
6 tbsp. melted margarine	1 tsp. salt
3 c. bread crumbs	3/4 tsp. monosodium glutamate
1/2 c. diced celery	1/8 tsp. pepper
1/3 c. chopped onion	

Brush the chicken breasts with 2 tablespoons margarine. Combine remaining margarine and remaining ingredients in a bowl. Place in mounds on 4 squares of double aluminum foil and place the foil in a baking sheet. Place chicken breasts, skin side up, on stuffing and fold foil securely around chicken. Bake at 350 degrees for 40 minutes. Increase temperature to 400 degrees and fold back the foil. Bake for 10 minutes longer or until chicken is brown.

Jane Sturgeon, Durham, North Carolina

SUNDAY DINNER SPECIAL

1 4-oz. can shredded coconut	1/2 tsp. crushed red pepper
2 tbsp. salad oil	2 tsp. grated lemon peel
1 tbsp. butter	1/2 tsp. sugar
4 chicken breasts, split	Sliced scallions
1/2 c. salted peanuts	1 tbsp. soy sauce
2 cloves of garlic	2 16-oz. cans Louisiana
Salt	yams, drained
1 tsp. ground coriander	2 tbsp. cornstarch

Combine 2 cups water and the coconut and let stand for 30 minutes. Heat the oil and butter together in a large skillet, then add the chicken and brown on all sides. Combine the peanuts, garlic, 1 teaspoon salt, spices, lemon peel and sugar in an electric blender and blend until peanuts are finely chopped. Drain the coconut and add the coconut milk to the peanut mixture, then stir in 1/3 cup scallions and the soy sauce. Add to the chicken, then cover and simmer for 20 minutes or until chicken is tender. Add the yams and cook for 5 minutes longer. Remove the chicken and yams to a serving dish and keep warm. Blend 2 tablespoons water and the cornstarch together, then stir into the cooking liquid. Cook and stir until sauce boils for 1 minute, then add salt to taste and pour over the chicken and yams. Toss 1/4 cup scallions and 1/4 cup of the coconut and sprinkle over the chicken. Garnish with lemon slices. 4 servings.

Sunday Dinner Special (above)

69

ROAST TURKEY WITH DRESSING

1 8 to 10-lb. turkey	3 c. crumbled corn bread
Salt	1 1/2 c. chopped hard-cooked
1 1/2 c. chopped celery	eggs
1/3 c. chopped onion	1/4 tsp. pepper
4 c. crumbled toast or biscuit	1/3 c. margarine

Preheat oven to 325 degrees. Brush the turkey with fat and season inside and out with salt. Place, breast side up, in a baking pan and add about 1 inch water to pan. Cover pan with foil. Bake for 4 hours to 4 hours and 30 minutes. Drain and reserve broth. Place the celery and onion in a saucepan and cover with boiling water. Simmer until tender and do not drain. Combine breads in a large bowl. Add the celery mixture, eggs, pepper, 1 1/2 teaspoons salt and enough turkey broth to moisten and mix well. Stir in the margarine and place in a greased pan. Bake at 350 degrees for about 25 minutes and serve with giblet gravy, if desired.

Mrs. Homer Shell, Piedmont, Alabama

CHARCOALED DOVE

1/2 c. melted margarine	1 pod of red pepper, chopped
1 c. vinegar	20 dove

Combine the margarine, vinegar and red pepper in a bowl. Dip the dove in the vinegar mixture and place on a grill over hot coals. Cook until tender and brown, basting with vinegar mixture frequently.

Genevieve B. Barnes, New Bern, North Carolina

STUFFED QUAIL

1/2 c. bulk sausage	1/8 tsp. pepper
1/2 c. diced celery	1/2 tsp. sage
1 1/2 c. crumbled corn bread	3/4 c. hot water
1/2 c. chopped tart apples	6 quail
1/4 tsp. salt	1 tbsp. melted butter

Cook the sausage and celery in a skillet until light brown, stirring frequently. Add remaining ingredients except quail and butter and mix well. Stuff the quail with sausage mixture and truss. Rub with butter and place in a roaster. Cover. Bake at 325 degrees for 1 hour and 40 minutes. Remove cover and bake for 20 minutes longer.

Mrs. Anne M. Carter, Millus Creek, North Carolina

SOUTH CAROLINA SHRIMP CASSEROLE

1/2 lb. mushrooms, sliced	2 tbsp. butter
1 onion, minced	1 lge. can tomatoes

3 tbsp. flour
1 c. chicken stock
1/2 c. milk
1/2 c. sherry

1 tbsp. Worcestershire sauce
Salt and pepper to taste
3 lb. cleaned cooked shrimp
Buttered crumbs

Saute the mushrooms and onion in butter in a saucepan until tender. Add the tomatoes and simmer for 10 minutes. Blend the flour with small amount of the stock, then stir in remaining stock. Stir into the tomato mixture. Stir in the milk, sherry, Worcestershire sauce, salt, pepper and shrimp. Place in a large, greased casserole and cover with crumbs. Bake at 350 degrees for about 30 minutes. 6 servings.

Mrs. Harold M. Allison, Greenville, South Carolina

SAVORY SHRIMP IN BUTTERED BREAD CRUMBS

1 peeled carrot, chopped
2 celery tops
2 sprigs of parsley
5 peppercorns
1 bay leaf
Salt
1   12-oz. package frozen
    shrimp, deveined

1/2 c. butter or margarine
1/2 clove of garlic, minced
1 med. onion, minced
1/2 c. fine dry bread crumbs
Juice of 1 lemon
2 tsp. minced parsley
Pepper to taste

Place 1 quart water in a saucepan. Add the carrot, celery tops, parsley, peppercorns, bay leaf and 1 tablespoon salt, then bring to a boil. Add the shrimp. Bring to a boil and cook for 1 minute more. Remove from heat and cool in stock for at least 2 hours. Drain. Melt the butter in a serving skillet over moderate heat and add the garlic, onion and bread crumbs. Toss over low heat until the onion is tender, but not browned. Add the shrimp, lemon juice and 1 teaspoon minced parsley and stir until heated through. Season with salt and pepper. Garnish with the remaining parsley. 3 servings.

Savory Shrimp in Buttered Bread Crumbs (above)

CAROLINA SHRIMP PIE

2 lb. shrimp	1/2 tsp. pepper
2 c. cracker crumbs	1/2 c. melted margarine
1/2 tbsp. salt	3 c. half and half

Cook the shrimp in boiling salted water for 10 minutes, then drain. Peel and devein. Place alternate layers of cracker crumbs, shrimp, salt, pepper and margarine in a casserole, ending with crumbs, then pour the half and half over top. Bake at 375 degrees for about 30 minutes or until light brown.

Mrs. Sara Brunson George, Florence, South Carolina

CRAB AND WILD RICE

1/2 lb. wild rice	2 4-oz. cans mushrooms,
1 can mushroom soup	drained
1/2 c. light cream	1 c. grated cheese
1 1/2 lb. crab meat	

Cook the rice according to package directions. Dilute the soup with cream. Layer the rice, crab meat, soup mixture, mushrooms and cheese in a greased casserole and cover. Bake at 350 degrees for 30 minutes. Uncover and bake until cheese is melted. 8 servings.

Byanthia Retherford, Pace, Florida

DEVILED CRAB CASSEROLE

1 c. milk	1/3 tsp. dry mustard
1 c. soft bread crumbs	1/2 tsp. lemon juice
2 c. cooked flaked crab	1/8 tsp. cayenne pepper
meat	1/4 c. melted margarine
2 hard-boiled eggs, mashed	Buttered bread crumbs
1 1/2 tsp. salt	

Combine the milk and bread crumbs in a bowl and stir in the crab meat and eggs. Blend in remaining ingredients except crumbs. Place in a greased 10 x 6 x 2-inch baking dish and cover with buttered crumbs. Bake in 400-degree oven for 15 minutes. 6 servings.

Camille B. Clarke, Greenville, North Carolina

BROILED SCALLOPS

1 qt. scallops	2 tbsp. dry mustard
Fine bread crumbs	6 drops of Worcestershire
2 eggs, beaten	sauce
1/2 c. melted butter	2 tbsp. water
4 bacon strips	

Wash the scallops and drain thoroughly. Dip in crumbs. Dip in the eggs, then in crumbs again. Place in a baking dish and pour half the butter over scallops. Arrange the bacon strips on scallops. Broil for about 6 minutes or until bacon is partially done. Turn the bacon and broil for about 6 minutes longer or until bacon is crisp. Mix the mustard, Worcestershire sauce and water in a saucepan until mustard is dissolved. Add remaining butter and heat through. Serve with scallops.

Mrs. Russell A. McMillan, Winter Haven, Florida

CATFISH AND POTATOES

1 1-lb. freshwater catfish	Salt and pepper to taste
2 med. potatoes, sliced	Butter
1 sm. onion, sliced	Catsup (opt.)

Preheat oven to 350 degrees. Place the catfish on a sheet of heavy-duty foil and place the potatoes around the catfish. Arrange onion on catfish and potatoes and sprinkle with salt and pepper. Dot with butter. Fold the foil over, seal and place in a baking pan. Bake for 50 minutes. Open the foil and drizzle the catfish mixture with catsup. Bake for 10 minutes longer.

Mrs. Nancy Roberson, Bristol, Florida

FISH ROE CAKES

1 8-oz. can fish roe	1/2 tsp. lemon juice
2 med. eggs, beaten	Pinch of salt
1 c. cracker crumbs	

Combine the fish roe and liquid with remaining ingredients and mix well. Shape into patties. Brown in small amount of bacon fat, turning once. Place on a platter and garnish with crisp bacon and lemon wedges. 2-4 servings.

Mrs. Howard F. Godfrey, Fayetteville, North Carolina

PAN-FRIED FISH FILLETS

2 lb. fish fillets	1 tbsp. milk or water
1 tsp. salt	1 c. fine dry bread crumbs
1 egg, slightly beaten	Cooking oil

Cut the fillets into serving pieces and sprinkle with salt. Mix the egg and milk in a shallow dish. Dip the fillets in egg mixture, then in bread crumbs. Heat about 1/8 inch oil in a skillet. Add the fillets and cook over medium heat until brown. Reduce heat and cook for 10 minutes or until fish flakes easily when tested with a fork. Drain on absorbent paper. 6 servings.

Wanda June Helms, Magnolia, Arkansas

STUFFED FISH ROLL-UPS

6 strips bacon	1/2 tsp. poultry seasoning
1/2 c. fine bread crumbs	6 sole fillets
10 scallions, minced	Melted butter
2 tbsp. chopped parsley	1 can cream of mushroom soup
1/2 lb. cooked scallops,	1/3 c. cream or milk
chopped	2 tbsp. capers
1 c. chopped apples	

Fry the bacon in a skillet until crisp. Remove from skillet and drain. Reserve 1/4 cup bacon drippings. Combine the crumbs, scallions, parsley, scallops, apples, poultry seasoning and reserved bacon drippings and mix well. Spread fillets with scallop mixture and roll up. Place close together, seam side down, in a foil-lined baking dish. Bake at 375 degrees for 30 minutes. Brush with melted butter, then broil until brown. Mix the mushroom soup, cream and capers in a saucepan and heat through. Serve with the sole. 6 servings.

Mrs. Vernon Spiers, Raleigh, North Carolina

LOBSTER THERMIDOR

4 8-oz. frozen rock	1 tsp. salt
lobster-tails	1/2 tsp. celery salt
Vinegar	Dash of cayenne pepper
4 tbsp. butter or margarine	2 egg yolks, slightly
4 tbsp. flour	beaten
1/2 tsp. prepared mustard	2 tsp. lemon juice
1 1/2 c. milk	1/4 to 1/3 c. sherry
1 c. heavy cream	Buttered crumbs
1/2 tsp. grated onion	

Drop the lobster-tails into boiling water, adding 1 tablespoon vinegar for each quart of water. Bring to a boil and cook for 11 minutes. Drain, then rinse with cold water. Cut away thin shell on underside and remove lobster meat. Cut into small pieces. Reserve outer shells. Melt the butter over low heat. Blend in the flour and cook until bubbly. Add the mustard and remove from heat. Stir in the milk gradually and cook, stirring constantly, until thickened. Add the cream, onion, salt, celery salt and cayenne pepper. Blend small amount of hot sauce into egg yolks, then stir back into hot sauce. Stir in the lemon juice, sherry and lobster meat. Fill reserved shells with lobster mixture and sprinkle with buttered crumbs. Place on a baking sheet. Brown lightly under broiler.

Celia Stansbury, Asheville, North Carolina

SCALLOPED CORN AND OYSTERS

1 pt. oysters	1 qt. fresh-cut corn,
2 c. coarse cracker crumbs	cooked
1/2 tsp. salt	1 tsp. Worcestershire sauce
1/4 tsp. pepper	1 c. milk
1/2 c. melted butter	

Drain the oysters and reserve liquid. Combine the cracker crumbs, salt, pepper and butter. Sprinkle 1/3 of the crumb mixture in a well-buttered casserole and cover with 1/2 of the oysters and 1/2 of the corn. Repeat layers. Mix the Worcestershire sauce, reserved liquid and milk and pour over casserole. Sprinkle with remaining crumbs. Bake in 350-degree oven for 30 minutes, adding milk, if needed.

Mrs. O. W. Watson, Rock Hill, South Carolina

ASPARAGUS SPEARS WITH SHRIMP SAUCE

2 sm. bunches fresh asparagus	Dash of paprika
1/4 c. butter	2 c. milk
1/4 c. flour	1 1/2 c. cooked shrimp,
1 tsp. salt	deveined
Dash of pepper	2 hard-cooked eggs, sliced
Dash of hot sauce	6 slices buttered toast

Break the tender part of each asparagus spear from woody base and remove scales. Wash thoroughly. Cook, covered, in salted boiling water until tender, then drain. Melt the butter in a saucepan over low heat and blend in flour and seasonings. Add the milk slowly, stirring constantly, until sauce is smooth and thickened. Fold the shrimp and eggs into the sauce carefully and heat through. Place the hot toast slices on a serving dish and cover with asparagus spears. Top with the shrimp sauce or pour sauce in separate dish to be served with the asparagus. Garnish with pimento and sprigs of parsley. Serve with broiled tomatoes. 6 servings.

Asparagus Spears with Shrimp Sauce (above)

BEETS WITH HONEY SAUCE

2 tbsp. melted butter	2 tbsp. light brown sugar
2 tbsp. flour	2 tsp. lemon juice
1 tbsp. honey	3 c. cooked beets

Melt the butter in a saucepan and blend in flour. Add remaining ingredients except beets and simmer until thickened and clear. Add the beets and heat through.

Maude E. Ramsdell, Durham, North Carolina

COLLARD GREENS

1/3 lb. salt meat	1 bunch collards

Wash the salt meat and score to the rind. Place in a large saucepan and add about 1 inch boiling water. Cook until tender. Wash the collards until clean and add to the saucepan. Cook until greens are tender, adding water, if needed. Chop greens well before serving.

Mrs. Margaret Betsworth, Pensacola, Florida

DANDELIONS SAUTEED WITH GARLIC

2 lb. fresh dandelion greens	2 cloves of garlic, chopped
4 tbsp. olive oil	Salt and pepper to taste

Clean the dandelion greens thoroughly, then cut in large pieces. Heat the oil and garlic in a saucepan. Add the greens, salt and pepper and cook for about 12 minutes or until tender, stirring frequently and adding water, if necessary. Serve hot. 4 servings.

Mildred Sasser, Spartanburg, South Carolina

OKRA PILAU

4 bacon slices, chopped	1 c. long grain rice
2 c. sliced okra	Salt and pepper to taste
1 1/2 c. water	

Cook the bacon in a saucepan until almost crisp. Add the okra and cook until tender. Add the water, rice, salt and pepper and cover. Cook over low heat, stirring occasionally, for about 1 hour or until rice is tender and liquid absorbed. 4-6 servings.

Mrs. N. G. Sires, Jr., Isle of Palms, South Carolina

GREEN BEANS WITH HERB BUTTER

1 lb. green beans	2 tbsp. sesame seed
1/4 c. butter or margarine	1/4 tsp. rosemary
3/4 c. minced onions	1/4 tsp. dried basil
1 clove of garlic, minced	3/4 tsp. salt
1/4 c. minced celery	1/2 c. snipped parsley

Wash and trim the beans, then cut crosswise into diagonal slices. Cook beans, covered, in 1/2 inch boiling, salted water for 15 minutes or until tender, then drain. Melt the butter in a saucepan. Add the onions, garlic, celery and sesame seed and saute for 5 minutes. Add remaining ingredients and cover. Simmer for 10 minutes. Add to the beans and mix well. 4 servings.

Jo Anna Littrel, Fort Meyers Beach, Florida

REBEL YELL FRIED GRITS

2 tsp. salt	1 egg, lightly beaten
1 c. grits	1/2 c. flour
Butter	

Bring 5 cups water and the salt to a boil in a heavy 2-quart saucepan over high heat. Stir in the grits slowly so that the water continues to boil. Reduce heat and cover. Cook, stirring occasionally, for 30 minutes. Stir in 1 tablespoon butter and spoon into a greased 9 x 13-inch baking dish. Smooth the top and cool to room temperature. Cover with foil and refrigerate for at least 4 hours. Cut the grits into 2-inch squares with a sharp knife. Mix the egg with 2 tablespoons cold water. Dip the grits in egg mixture, then roll in the flour. Melt 4 tablespoons butter in a heavy 12-inch skillet over moderate heat. Add 7 or 8 of the grits squares and cook for about 3 minutes on each side or until brown, turning with a spatula. Remove from skillet and keep warm. Repeat with remaining grits squares, adding butter to the skillet as needed. Place on a heated platter and serve.

Naurene Hammond, Beaufort, South Carolina

SPRING RICE FESTIVAL

3 green onions with tops, chopped	2 c. cooked rice
2 tbsp. butter or shortening	Salt and pepper to taste
	2 eggs, well beaten

Saute the onions in butter in a saucepan until tender. Add rice, salt and pepper and mix well. Blend in eggs. Place in a casserole and set casserole in pan of water. Bake at 325 degrees for 30 minutes or until set.

Mrs. Lola Hopkins, Mardela, Maryland

SWEET POTATO AND APPLE CASSEROLE

6 fresh sweet potatoes	Dash of salt
3 apples	1 c. water
1 c. (packed) brown sugar	4 pork chops, fat removed
3 tbsp. butter or margarine	

Wash the potatoes and place in a saucepan. Cover with water and bring to a boil. Reduce heat and simmer until tender. Drain and cool. Peel and cut into 1/2-inch slices. Peel, core and slice the apples. Place alternate layers of potato and apple slices in a casserole. Mix the brown sugar, butter, salt and water in a saucepan and cook to light-syrup stage, stirring constantly. Pour over potatoes and apples and place pork chops on top. Bake at 350 degrees until pork chops are well done and apples are tender.

Mrs. J. Norris Hanning, New Orleans, Louisiana

HEIRLOOM SWEET POTATO BISCUITS

2 c. flour	1/2 c. shortening
2/3 c. sugar	2 c. mashed cooked sweet
2 tbsp. baking powder	potatoes
1 1/2 tsp. salt	1/4 c. milk

Sift the flour, sugar, baking powder and salt together into a bowl and cut in the shortening until mixture is consistency of cornmeal. Stir in the sweet potatoes and milk. Turn out on floured board and knead lightly. Roll out to 1/2-inch thickness and cut with biscuit cutter. Place on a greased cookie sheet. Bake at 425 degrees for 12 to 15 minutes. 2 dozen.

Mrs. Alta P. Addis, Gaffney, South Carolina

BRIOCHE WITH RUM-FRUIT

1 pkg. yeast	1 egg yolk
3 c. sifted flour	1 c. apricot jam
2 eggs	1/2 c. sliced toasted almonds
2 1/2 tbsp. sugar	2 c. cooked mixed fruits
1/4 tsp. salt	1 1/2 tbsp. rum
9 tbsp. soft butter	

Dissolve the yeast in 1/2 cup lukewarm water in a bowl. Add 1 cup flour and mix well. Place remaining flour in a large bowl and make a well in the center. Place the eggs, sugar, salt and yeast mixture in the well. Add the butter and mix until smooth. Cover and let rise for about 1 hour or until doubled in bulk. Punch down and reserve 1/4 of the dough for top. Roll the remaining dough into a large ball and place in a greased fluted mold. Roll reserved dough in the shape of a pear and punch the pointed end into mixture in mold. Cover and let rise for about 30 minutes or until doubled in bulk. Make an indentation around top ball of dough with a sharp knife to separate slightly from the base of the Brioche.

Bake in a 425-degree oven for 30 minutes. Brush the top of the Brioche with egg yolk mixed with a small amount of water and bake for 5 minutes longer or until Brioche tests done. Remove top ball by cutting around the indentation and set aside. Scoop out part of the inner portion of the Brioche. Spread half the jam in the shell and sprinkle with almonds. Mix remaining jam, fruits and rum and fill the shell. Replace top and slice in wedges to serve.

Mrs. Ed Riley, Mobile, Alabama

SPICY BLUEBERRY PANCAKES

2 c. packaged biscuit mix	1/2 tsp. nutmeg
1 egg	1/4 tsp. cloves
1 2/3 c. milk	1 c. drained blueberries
1 tsp. cinnamon	

Place the biscuit mix, egg and milk in a bowl and beat with a rotary beater until smooth. Add the spices and blueberries and mix well. Drop by spoonfuls onto a hot, greased griddle and cook until brown on both sides, turning once. Serve with syrup.

Belle Stanley, Knoxville, Tennessee

CRISPY CORN FRITTERS

1 7-oz. can whole kernel corn	2 tbsp. minced green pepper
Milk	1 tbsp. minced pimento
1 1/2 c. pancake mix	2 eggs, separated

Drain the corn, reserving the liquid. Add enough milk to the reserved liquid to make 3/4 cup. Combine the pancake mix, corn, green pepper and pimento in medium-sized bowl, then add the milk mixture and beaten egg yolks. Blend well. Fold in the stiffly beaten egg whites. Drop by tablespoonfuls into deep fat at 375 degrees, turning when brown on underside. Fry about 3 minutes or until golden brown. Drain on absorbent paper. Serve with maple-blended syrup. 2 dozen.

Crispy Corn Fritters (above)

SWEET POTATO ROLLS

1 c. cooked sweet potatoes	1 1/2 tsp. salt
3 tbsp. butter or margarine	3 tbsp. sugar
1 pkg. dry yeast	5 c. sifted flour
1 egg, beaten	Melted butter

Mix the potatoes and margarine in a bowl. Dissolve the yeast in 1/2 cup warm water, then stir into potato mixture. Add the egg, salt and sugar and mix well. Add flour alternately with 3/4 cup warm water. Turn onto a well-floured board and knead. Place in a greased bowl and cover. Let rise for 2 hours or until doubled in bulk. Place on a floured board and roll out. Cut with a small biscuit cutter and place on a greased cookie sheet. Brush tops of rolls with melted butter and let rise for 1 hour or until doubled in bulk. Bake in 425-degree oven for 15 to 20 minutes. 30 rolls.

Mable Henderson, Tahlequah, Oklahoma

BLUEBERRY COFFEE CAKE

1/2 c. shortening	1/4 tsp. salt
1 1/4 c. sugar	1/2 c. milk
1 egg, well beaten	2 c. blueberries
2 1/2 c. sifted flour	1/2 tsp. cinnamon
2 1/2 tsp. baking powder	1/4 c. butter or margarine

Cream the shortening and 3/4 cup sugar in a bowl. Add the egg and mix well. Sift 2 cups flour with baking powder and salt and add to creamed mixture alternately with milk. Place in a well-greased 11 1/2 x 7 1/2 x 1 1/2-inch pan and sprinkle with blueberries. Combine remaining sugar, cinnamon and remaining flour in a bowl and cut in the butter until mixture resembles crumbs. Sprinkle over blueberries. Bake in 350-degree oven for 45 to 50 minutes. Cut in squares and serve warm with cream, if desired. 8-10 servings.

Mrs. Lillian Hall, Florence, Alabama

GRANDMOTHER'S DOUGHNUTS

1/2 c. mashed potatoes	2 1/2 tsp. baking powder
3/4 c. sugar	1/2 tsp. salt
1 egg	1/2 tsp. nutmeg
1/2 c. milk	Powdered sugar
2 c. flour	

Combine the potatoes, sugar, egg and milk in a bowl. Sift the flour, baking powder, salt and nutmeg together and stir into the sugar mixture. Roll out on a floured surface and cut with a doughnut cutter. Drop into deep, hot fat and fry until golden brown. Drain and roll in powdered sugar. 3 dozen.

Mrs. Paul Katonak, Aiken, South Carolina

PEANUT YEAST BREAD

1 pkg. dry yeast
1 1/4 c. warm water
1/4 c. crunchy peanut butter
1/4 c. chopped peanuts

2 tsp. salt
1/4 c. (packed) brown sugar
3 c. flour

Dissolve the yeast in warm water in a bowl. Add peanut butter, peanuts, salt, brown sugar and 1 1/2 cups flour and beat with electric mixer at medium speed for 2 minutes. Add remaining flour and stir until smooth. Cover and let rise until doubled in bulk. Beat for 25 strokes. Place in well-buttered 9 x 5 x 2-inch pan and cover. Let rise until dough is 1 inch above top of pan. Bake at 375 degrees for 45 minutes or until brown. Remove from pan and place on a rack to cool.

Mrs. Vonzeal Tubbs, Darden, Tennessee

MOONSHINE WHISKEY CAKE

1/2 c. butter
1 c. sugar
3 eggs, beaten
1 3/4 c. (about) flour
1/2 tsp. baking powder
1/4 tsp. salt
1/2 tsp. nutmeg

1/4 c. milk
1/4 tsp. soda
1/4 c. molasses
1 lb. seedless raisins
2 c. chopped pecans or
    walnuts
1/4 c. bourbon

Cream the butter and sugar in a bowl, then stir in the eggs. Mix the flour, baking powder, salt and nutmeg and stir into the butter mixture. Stir in the milk. Mix the soda with molasses and stir into the butter mixture. Stir in the raisins, pecans and bourbon and pour into greased and floured loaf pans. Bake at 300 degrees for 2 hours. Cool and remove from pans. Wrap in foil and store in refrigerator.

Sherree Norwood, Columbia, South Carolina

CREME BRULEE

1/2 c. sugar
4 egg yolks, beaten
4 tbsp. cornstarch
Pinch of salt

1 tbsp. vanilla
2 c. non-dairy coffee creamer
3 c. boiling water
1 1/2 c. confectioners' sugar

Combine the sugar, egg yolks, cornstarch, salt, vanilla and coffee creamer in a saucepan and mix well. Stir in boiling water slowly. Cook over medium heat for 3 to 5 minutes or until thickened, stirring constantly. Place pan in cold water and stir until cool. Pour into a bowl. Place confectioners' sugar in a large skillet and stir over moderate heat until melted. Pour over custard and chill. 6-8 servings.

Nancy Proctor, Salley, South Carolina

INDIAN SUMMER HARVEST CAKE

1 1/2 c. salad oil	1 tsp. nutmeg
2 c. sugar	4 tbsp. hot water
4 eggs, separated	1 1/2 c. grated sweet
2 1/2 c. sifted flour	potatoes
3 tsp. baking powder	1 c. chopped nuts
1/4 tsp. cinnamon	1 tsp. vanilla

Combine the oil and sugar in a bowl and beat until smooth. Add the egg yolks and beat well. Sift dry ingredients together. Stir water into sugar mixture, then stir in dry ingredients. Stir in potatoes, nuts and vanilla and beat well. Fold in stiffly beaten egg whites and pour into 3 greased 8-inch layer pans. Bake at 350 degrees for 25 to 30 minutes. Cool for 10 minutes and remove from pans. Cool on racks.

Frosting

1 lge. can evaporated milk	1 1/3 c. flaked coconut
1 c. sugar	1 tsp. vanilla
3 egg yolks	Chopped nuts to taste (opt.)
1 stick margarine	

Combine the milk, sugar, egg yolks and margarine in a double boiler and cook until thick, stirring occasionally. Remove from heat and stir in coconut, vanilla and nuts. Spread between layers and on top and side of cake.

Mrs. Thaney Self, Hornbeck, Louisiana

CHARLOTTE RUSSE

3/4 tbsp. unflavored gelatin	1 c. heavy cream, whipped
1/3 c. scalded milk	1 c. chopped peaches or berries
1/3 c. confectioners' sugar	6 ladyfingers, split
1 1/2 tsp. vanilla	

Soften the gelatin in 1/4 cup cold water, then stir into the milk until dissolved. Strain into a bowl and add the confectioners' sugar and vanilla. Set the bowl in ice water and chill, stirring constantly, until thickened. Beat until fluffy, then beat in 1/3 of the whipped cream. Fold in the remaining whipped cream and add the peaches. Line a mold with ladyfingers and fill with the peach mixture. Chill until firm. Garnish with additional whipped cream. 6 servings.

Mrs. Nathalie Cook, Radford, Virginia

BLUEBERRY PIE DELUXE

4 c. fresh blueberries	Juice of 1/2 lemon
1 c. water	1 c. heavy cream
Sugar	1 baked pie shell, cooled
3 tbsp. cornstarch	

Mix 1 cup blueberries with water and 1 cup sugar in a saucepan and bring to a boil. Reduce heat and simmer until blueberries are tender. Strain the liquid and discard blueberries. Bring the blueberry liquid to a boil. Mix the cornstarch with 1/4 cup water. Stir into the boiling liquid and cook, stirring, until thick. Place remaining blueberries in a large bowl and add lemon juice. Pour hot mixture over the blueberries and cool. Whip the cream until stiff, adding sugar to taste, then spoon into the pie shell. Pour the blueberry mixture over the whipped cream and chill for several hours.

Mrs. Marie Capps, Sumter, South Carolina

APRICOT FLAN

1 30-oz. can apricot halves	4 tbsp. Grand Marnier
1 pkg. vanilla pudding and pie filling mix	1 baked 10-in. pie shell
	4 red maraschino cherry halves
1 c. heavy cream	2 tbsp. sugar
1 egg, beaten	1 tbsp. cornstarch

Drain the apricots, reserving 1 1/4 cups syrup, then chill the apricots. Blend the pie filling mix, cream, egg and 1/2 cup of the reserved syrup in a medium saucepan, then bring to a boil over medium heat, stirring constantly. Remove from heat and cool slightly, then stir in 3 tablespoons Grand Marnier. Beat the custard mixture until smooth. Spoon into pie shell and chill for at least 1 hour. Slice all but 4 of the apricot halves. Space the 4 apricot halves evenly around edge of pie filling, then form 4 apricot flowers between the halves with the slices. Place a cherry half in center of each flower. Blend the sugar and cornstarch together in a small saucepan, then stir in the remaining apricot syrup. Boil for 1 minute, stirring constantly. Remove from heat and stir in the remaining Grand Marnier. Spoon the warm glaze over fruit and pie filling. Chill until serving time.

Apricot Flan (above)

favorite foods of tennessee and kentucky

It was in Tennessee and Kentucky that the westward and southward movement to populate the Deep South was first made. Attracted by tales of fast, well-watered expanses filled with herds of game and fertile fields, frontiersmen and their families pushed through mountain passes to settle this section. They traveled light, with all the family's furniture and household equipment usually confined to one covered wagon. And among that equipment was certain to be an iron pot, a heavy skillet, and at least a few carefully preserved "receipts." With these slender assets, the pioneer woman would help feed her family in the strange new land ahead.

Many of these recipes have come down through pioneer families and their neighbors to form an important part of Deep South cookery. Some of the best are included in the section that follows. Look, for example, at recipes like Chicken Lima Stew, Braised Shanks with Cornmeal Dumplings, Turnip Greens also with Cornmeal Dumplings, and Homemade Sausage. You can almost see and smell these hearty and wholesome foods simmering in an iron pot suspended over the fire that both heated the family and cooked its food.

As you browse through these pages, you are certain to discover modern, easy to prepare versions of foods that will be as appreciated by your family as they were by those pioneer families of long ago.

ennessee and Kentucky were once considered the western frontier of the American colonies. Kentucky was a region sacred to and feared by the numerous Indian tribes of the interior. They roamed through it and hunted in it but none, not even the almost fearless Tuscarora, called it home. Tennessee, in contrast, was the home of the Cherokee and Creek tribes who were, until the mid-1700's, strongly resistent to any settlement by the white men.

HISTORY AND TRADITIONS OF

tennessee
and kentucky

But settle the white men did, in both Tennessee and Kentucky. Pioneer families from Virginia and the Carolinas and emigrants from Scotland, Ireland, and Germany crossed the Blue Ridge Mountains, traversed the Shenandoah Valley to the north or south, then crossed the Allegheny Mountains to reach Kentucky and Tennessee. Here they established struggling settlements on the sides of the mountains, in hollows, and, later, along the prairie lands of western Kentucky and Tennessee. Two very different kinds of people emerged from these settlements: one was the near-legendary mountain folk who echoed in their speech patterns, songs, customs, and foods the lands from which they came. The other group were the plantation owners. Located primarily in the fertile western prairie regions, these were people for whom tobacco or horse raising provided sufficient funds to raise gracious Georgian or Greek revival mansions and to establish a lifestyle not unlike that of tidewater Virginia, Maryland, and South Carolina.

Whether mountain folk or plantation owner, one look at their dining tables would be sufficient to establish their common origins. Both featured ham, prominently. Especially popular was country ham, ham locally cured using immediately available wood to provide smoke. Each small section had its own flavor of country ham and, some claimed, you could travel hundreds of miles throughout Tennessee and Kentucky without tasting the same kind of ham twice! Both plantation and mountain tables featured corn, too. Corn was served as a vegetable, in many different kinds of bread, and in the liquor that later was known as bourbon. Another food that indicated the common beginnings of both groups was greens. Greens were frequently served throughout the South, but in Tennessee and Kentucky emerged the custom of cooking greens with a bit of ham, pork, or "fat back" for flavoring.

Today, throughout the Southland, most greens served carry this flavoring with them.

THE BEGINNINGS

No name is perhaps so prominent in the settlement of Tennessee and Kentucky as is that of Daniel Boone. In 1752, Boone was living with his family in the western reaches of Virginia when John Finley, a buffalo hunter, brought him word of a wondrous land lying west of Ouesioto or the Cumberland Gap. This land was full of virgin hardwood forests, blue grass prairies, and fertile meadows. The wood could be transformed into houses, and the prairies and meadows into thriving farms. The huge flocks of turkey, ducks, and geese together with herds of buffalo and deer would provide plenty of food for the families adventuresome enough to risk everything to settle the new land. Best of all, this was not Indian land. It could be settled without the risk of perpetual attack.

Boone blazed what is now called the Wilderness Road, an incredibly beautiful and dangerous trail winding from Virginia through the Blue Ridge Mountains, down into the Shenandoah, and up again through the Alleghenys. The trail ended in Boonesboro, the first of the many Kentucky settlements.

While Boone was moving westward, another Virginia pioneer, William Bean was moving southwestward, toward Tennessee. In the Valley of the Watauga, a tributary of the Tennessee River, he established the first white settlement. It thrived despite repeated Indian attacks, and soon other smaller settlements spread out along other tributaries of the Tennessee.

This tiny movement westward was given impetus by two events. One was the migration of Europeans from Scotland, Ireland, and Germany. These newcomers were for the most part peasants eager for rich land and accustomed to hard work. These people were ideally suited for the frontier. Most of them landed in Philadelphia, then the only mid-Atlantic port capable of handling trans-Atlantic ships. Finding the land immediately around Philadelphia already settled, they were readily attracted by the prospect of new land and economic prosperity lying to the west. They poured through the Shenandoah Valley, some going due west to Kentucky while others, perhaps a bit more adventuresome, turned south, toward Tennessee.

The second event to give impetus to settlement in Tennessee and Kentucky was the American Revolution. Many people, eager to save their families from the turmoil of war, moved westward. Between the two movements, one away from war and the other away from Europe, the lands of Tennessee and Kentucky were populated, cultivated, and made to yield their riches. By the end of the 1700's, the frontier was no longer in these two regions but lay further to the south and west, in Alabama, Mississippi, Louisiana, and western Georgia.

Scotch Barley Soup (below)

SCOTCH BARLEY SOUP

2 lb. lamb neck slices	1 tsp. monosodium glutamate
2 ribs celery, sliced	1 lge. bay leaf
1 med. onion, sliced	1/2 c. pearl barley
1 clove of garlic, crushed	2 c. sliced carrots
2 1/2 tsp. salt	1 1/2 c. diced white turnips
1 tsp. peppercorns	1/2 c. sliced scallions

Combine the lamb, celery, onion, garlic, 2 teaspoons salt, peppercorns, monosodium glutamate, bay leaf and 2 quarts water in a Dutch oven. Bring to a boil, then cover tightly and simmer for 1 hour. Strain and remove excess fat from broth. Measure the broth and add enough water to measure 1 1/2 quarts. Return broth and lamb to the Dutch oven and bring to a boil. Stir in the barley and simmer, covered, for 30 minutes, stirring occasionally. Add the remaining salt, carrots and turnips and cook, covered, for 20 minutes. Stir in the scallions and simmer, covered, for 10 minutes longer. Turn into soup tureen and sprinkle with parsley, if desired. 6-8 servings.

HERB SOUP

3 No. 2 cans tomatoes	1/2 c. chopped onion
2 cans consomme	1 tbsp. salt
1/2 tsp. dried basil	1/8 tsp. white pepper
1/2 c. chopped celery	1 tbsp. margarine
4 whole cloves	1 tbsp. sugar

Combine all the ingredients in a kettle and cook until the vegetables are tender. Mash the vegetables with a potato masher. Serve with croutons and sour cream.

Mrs. Gertrude D. Lape, Little Rock, Arkansas

CHICKEN-LIMA STEW

1 chicken	1/2 tsp. salt
1 onion, minced	1/8 tsp. pepper
1 No. 2 can corn	1 can green lima beans
1 8 oz. can tomato sauce	2 potatoes, diced
1 tsp. Worcestershire sauce	1 tsp. lemon juice
1 tbsp. catsup	1/4 c. butter
Dash of hot sauce	

Place the chicken in a saucepan and cover with water. Add the onion. Bring to a boil and reduce heat. Simmer until chicken is tender. Remove chicken from broth and cool. Remove chicken from bones and place in broth. Add remaining ingredients and simmer for 1 hour, stirring frequently. 4 servings.

Mrs. Joe Rodgers, Nashville, Tennessee

CORN AND CHICKEN SOUP

1 c. canned corn	2 c. hot milk
1/2 c. minced celery	2 egg yolks, slightly beaten
1 c. minced cooked chicken	2 tbsp. butter
4 c. chicken stock	Salt and pepper to taste

Heat the corn and press through a coarse sieve. Add the corn pulp, celery and chicken to stock in a saucepan and bring to a boil. Cover. Simmer for 15 minutes. Stir the milk into egg yolks gradually and add to chicken mixture. Cook for 2 minutes, stirring constantly. Add the butter, salt and pepper and serve with croutons. 8 servings.

Mrs. Warren West, Las Cruces, New Mexico

TRADITIONAL FOURTH DAY CAMP STEW

1 6-lb. hen	2 cans cream-style corn
2 1/2 lb. stew beef	2 cans tomato soup
2 1/2 lb. fresh pork roast	1/2 lb. margarine
1 lb. dried lima beans	1 can tomato paste
5 lb. onions, chopped	Salt and pepper to taste
10 lb. potatoes	1 dried red pepper
4 cans tomatoes	

Place the hen, beef and pork in a large kettle and cover with water. Bring to a boil and reduce heat. Cover and simmer until tender. Remove meats from broth and cool. Reserve broth. Remove meats from bones and chop. Soak the beans overnight in enough water to cover. Drain and add to reserved broth. Add the onions and cook until beans are tender. Peel the potatoes and dice. Mash the tomatoes. Add the meats, potatoes and tomatoes to bean mixture. Add remaining ingredients and cook, stirring frequently, until potatoes are done and stew is thickened. May be canned or frozen. 13 quarts.

Mrs. Ed Richey, Huntsville, Alabama

CHICKEN AND VEGETABLE STEW

1 lge. fryer	1 pt. lima beans
1 qt. corn	2 med. onions, chopped
1 qt. tomatoes	Salt and pepper to taste
1 pt. sliced okra	

Place the chicken in a large kettle and add enough water to cover. Cook until tender. Remove chicken from broth and cool. Remove chicken from bones and cut in large cubes. Return chicken to broth and add remaining ingredients. Simmer until thick, stirring frequently. 6-8 servings.

Mrs. Euna Bowman, Pelahatchie, Mississippi

CLOVE TOMATOES

4 lb. fresh tomatoes	1/2 c. raisins, chopped
1 1/4 tsp. whole cloves	1/4 c. lemon juice
1/4 tsp. whole allspice	2 tsp. salt
4 c. sugar	

Drop the tomatoes into boiling water for 2 minutes or until skins can be easily peeled. Remove the stems and skins with the tip of a sharp knife. Dice the tomatoes and place in a large saucepan. Tie the cloves and allspice into a cheesecloth bag, add to the tomatoes, then add the remaining ingredients. Bring to a boil, then reduce the heat and simmer for 1 hour and 30 minutes to 2 hours or until thick, stirring occasionally. Remove the cheesecloth bag. Ladle immediately into hot sterilized jars, filling to within 1/2 inch of top. Seal immediately. 6 half-pint jars.

Clove Tomatoes (above)

WATERMELON RIND PICKLES

7 lb. watermelon rind	4 lb. sugar
1 tbsp. slaked lime	1 pt. vinegar
1 gal. water	2 sticks cinnamon

Peel and cut the rind into 1 1/2-inch pieces, then soak overnight in a mixture of lime and water. Wash several times, then place in a large cooking pot. Cover with water and cook until tender, then drain. Mix the sugar, vinegar and cinnamon and bring to a boil. Cool. Pour over the rind and let stand overnight. Bring to a boil and boil until the rind is transparent. Pack the rind into hot sterilized jars, then fill with hot syrup. Seal the jars. 4 quarts.

Mrs. Martha B. Godwin, Windsor, Virginia

COLORFUL FRUIT AND MELON SALAD

1/4 tsp. vanilla	1 cantaloupe or honeydew melon
2 tbsp. sugar	Lettuce
1/2 c. whipped cream	Maraschino cherries
1 can fruit cocktail, drained	

Fold the vanilla and sugar into whipped cream, then fold into fruit cocktail. Peel and slice the cantaloupe. Place slices of cantaloupe on lettuce leaves and fill centers with fruit mixture. Top each serving with a cherry.

Mrs. Geneva Gill Cooper, Monticello, Kentucky

CUCUMBER AND CHICKEN SALAD

4 c. cold diced chicken	3 hard-cooked eggs, chopped
1 1/2 c. chopped celery	1 tbsp. diced pimento
1/2 c. sliced cucumber	1 tsp. salt
1/4 c. French dressing	1/4 c. chopped parsley

Combine the chicken, celery and cucumber and toss lightly. Mix in the French dressing and chill thoroughly. Add the remaining ingredients and mix well. Serve on lettuce with a cooked dressing.

Mrs. Mary A. Walters, Bonnieville, Kentucky

POTATO SALAD

1 qt. cooked cubed potatoes	1/2 c. chopped sweet pickles
1 sm. onion, chopped	3 hard-cooked eggs, chopped
1/4 c. chopped celery	1/2 c. salad dressing

Combine all the ingredients in a bowl and mix well. Chill overnight.

Mrs. Aubrey W. Walker, Oxford, Mississippi

OLD-FASHIONED COLESLAW

1 c. sugar	1 lge. cabbage, shredded
1 c. vinegar	1 carrot, shredded
1 c. salad dressing	1/2 green pepper, shredded
1 tsp. salt	1/2 fresh cucumber, grated
2 tbsp. milk	

Combine the sugar, vinegar, salad dressing, salt and milk in mixing bowl and beat until blended. Combine the remaining ingredients in a large bowl and pour the dressing over all, then toss well. Let stand for at least 20 minutes, then cool in refrigerator. 12 servings.

Mrs. Rufus George, London, Kentucky

BRAISED SHANKS WITH CORNMEAL DUMPLINGS

3 lb. crosscut beef shank slices	3 tbsp. lard
Flour	1 egg
Salt	1/4 c. milk
Pepper to taste	1 tsp. baking powder
	1/2 c. cornmeal

Dredge the shank slices with flour, then season with salt and pepper. Brown on both sides in hot lard in a deep skillet. Add 1 cup water and cover, then simmer for 2 hours or until tender, adding water as needed. Beat the egg well in a bowl, then add the milk. Sift 1/2 cup flour, baking powder, 1/2 teaspoon salt and cornmeal together, then add to the milk mixture, blending well. Drop by table-spoonfuls on the shank slices. Cover tightly and cook for 12 to 15 minutes. Serve immediately.

Mrs. Jess James, New Market, Tennessee

BAKED COUNTRY HAM

1 country ham	Pepper to taste
Dark brown sugar to taste	

Soak the ham in enough cold water to cover for at least 24 hours, then drain. Scrub well and trim off hock end. Place in a large kettle and cover with water. Bring to a boil and reduce heat. Simmer for 20 minutes per pound. Remove from heat and let ham cool in broth. Drain. Remove rind from ham. Score the fat side and rub with brown sugar and pepper. Place in a roaster. Bake in 350-degree oven for 30 minutes.

Mrs. R. M. Nettles, St. Augustine, Florida

BARBECUED COON

1 12-lb. coon, cleaned	1 1/2 c. vinegar
Salt	Dash of pepper
1/2 lge. onion, sliced	Barbecue Sauce
2 tsp. red pepper	

Cover the coon with water in a roaster, then add 2 tablespoons salt, onion, red pepper and vinegar. Parboil until tender, then pour off the water, leaving just enough to prevent coon from sticking. Season with pepper and salt and baste with the Barbecue Sauce. Bake at 350 degrees for 30 to 40 minutes.

Barbecue Sauce

1 c. mayonnaise	1 tbsp. horseradish
1 6-oz. can tomato paste	1/2 tsp. hot sauce
1/4 c. vinegar	1 tsp. salt
3 tbsp. Worcestershire sauce	1/2 tsp. cayenne pepper
1 tbsp. chopped onion	1/2 tsp. pepper

Combine all ingredients and mix well.

Mrs. Virginia Weidemann, Sikeston, Missouri

QUAIL IN MUSHROOM SAUCE

6 quail	1 can milk
Shortening	Salt and pepper to taste
1 can mushroom soup	

Brown the quail in shortening, then remove the quail and pour off the shortening. Add the soup, milk, salt and pepper and blend. Add the quail and simmer until tender.

Mrs. Annette Carson, Jackson, Mississippi

FRIED RABBIT

1 rabbit	3 tbsp. oil or butter
3/4 c. flour	1 sm. onion, sliced
Salt and pepper to taste	

Clean the rabbit and soak in salted water to cover overnight. Cut into serving pieces. Combine the flour, salt and pepper in a paper bag, then add the rabbit and shake until coated. Brown in the hot oil in a heavy skillet, then cover with onion and add 1/2 cup water. Cover and steam until tender. 4 servings.

Mrs. Beverly Adams, Ashland, Kentucky

ROASTED OPOSSUM

1 2-lb. parboiled opossum	2 lb. sweet potatoes, sliced
1 bunch green onions, sliced	

Place the opossum in a small roaster with 1 cup water and the onions. Bake at 325 degrees for about 1 hour, basting occasionally with the pan juices. Place the sweet potatoes around opossum and bake for 15 to 20 minutes longer or until potatoes are done. 5 servings.

Mrs. Cottie G. Finch, De Land, Florida

BARBECUED PORK CHOPS

4 tbsp. minced onion	1/2 tsp. pepper or cayenne
1 c. tomato sauce or puree	pepper
1 c. water	1 tsp. paprika
3 tbsp. vinegar	1/4 tsp. cinnamon
2 tbsp. Worcestershire sauce	Dash of ground cloves
1 tsp. chili powder	6 pork chops
1 tsp. salt	Flour
1/2 tsp. celery seed (opt.)	Cooking oil

Combine first 12 ingredients in a saucepan and bring to boiling point. Dust the pork chops with flour and brown on both sides in small amount of cooking oil in a skillet. Place chops on grill and place 1 tablespoon sauce on each chop. Cook the chops, turning and adding sauce, until done. 6 servings.

Mrs. S. T. Stanton, Memphis, Tennessee

KENTUCKY-BAKED SPARERIBS

3 lb. spareribs	1 tsp. salt

Cut the ribs into serving pieces, then season with the salt. Place in a heavy pan. Bake at 325 degrees for 30 minutes. Drain off the fat and turn the ribs. Bake for 30 minutes longer or until crisp and brown. Serve with barbecue sauce, if desired. 4 servings.

Inez Raley, Cromwell, Kentucky

VALLEY FORGE PORK CHOPS

8 pork chops	1/4 c. brown sugar
3 tbsp. shortening	2 tbsp. flour
1/2 tsp. salt	1 c. hot water
1/2 tsp. sage	1/4 tsp. vinegar
4 apples, cored	1/2 c. seedless raisins

Brown the pork chops in hot shortening in a skillet. Remove chops and reserve fat. Place the chops in a baking dish and sprinkle with salt and sage. Slice the apples in rings and sprinkle with brown sugar. Place on the pork chops. Stir the flour into reserved fat. Stir in the water and vinegar and cook, stirring, until thickened. Add the raisins and pour over apples. Bake at 350 degrees for 1 hour. 8 servings.

Rita Lindsey, Horse Cave, Kentucky

GLAZED PORK LOIN WITH APRICOT SAUCE

1 4-lb. pork loin roast	1/4 c. light corn syrup
1 1-lb. 14-oz. can apricot halves	3 tbsp. vinegar
1/3 c. sugar	1/4 tsp. salt

1/8 tsp. pepper   1/8 tsp. ground cloves
1/8 tsp. mace

Have the butcher cut pork roast butterfly-style. Drain the apricots and reserve 1/2 cup syrup. Combine reserved syrup, sugar, corn syrup, vinegar, salt, pepper, mace and cloves in a saucepan. Bring to boiling point and cook for 3 minutes. Open the roast. Place 10 apricot halves on half the roast and secure apricots at front edge with wooden picks. Drizzle 3 tablespoons sauce over apricots. Fold roast over apricots and tie securely. Place in a shallow roasting pan and brush with sauce. Roast at 325 degrees for about 2 hours or until done, basting frequently with sauce. Add remaining apricot halves and simmer for 10 minutes. 6-8 servings.

Ann Elsie Schmetzer, Madisonville, Kentucky

GLAZED YAMS AND MINI HAM LOAVES

1 lb. ground ham   1/4 tsp. pepper
1 lb. pork sausage   3/4 c. milk
1/3 c. soft bread crumbs   1 egg, slightly beaten
2 tbsp. minced celery   1   16-oz. can whole cranberry
2 tbsp. minced onion   sauce
2 tbsp. minced parsley   1/2 c. dark corn syrup
1/4 tsp. nutmeg   1/8 tsp. ground cloves
1/4 tsp. thyme   4 cooked peeled Louisiana
1/2 tsp. salt   yams, sliced

Combine the ham, sausage, bread crumbs, seasonings, milk and egg. Mix well and shape into 6 round loaves. Place each loaf in an individual baking dish. Bake at 350 degrees for 25 to 30 minutes. Combine the cranberry sauce, corn syrup and cloves in a saucepan and cook over low heat, stirring, until the cranberry sauce melts and blends with the corn syrup. Add the yam slices and stir to coat well. Remove the ham loaves from oven when done and pour off the excess drippings. Spoon the yams around each loaf. Spoon remaining cranberry glaze over loaves. Return the loaves to oven and bake for 5 to 10 minutes or until tops of loaves are glazed.

Glazed Yams and Mini Ham Loaves (above)

95

HOMEMADE SAUSAGE

6 lb. lean pork	2 tsp. cloves
3 lb. pork fat	2 tsp. mace
4 tbsp. sage	1 whole nutmeg, grated
2 tbsp. pepper	1 tbsp. pepper
2 tbsp. salt	1 tbsp. cayenne pepper (opt.)

Grind the pork through a sausage grinder 2 times, then add the remaining ingredients and mix well. Shape into patties and place on baking sheets. Freeze, then place in freezer bags and seal. Remove from freezer and thaw, then fry until browned on both sides.

Mrs. Edgar W. Greene, Minter, Alabama

SAUSAGE-POTATO CASSEROLE

Sliced potatoes	Sliced smoked sausage
Sliced onions	1 can tomato soup
1 lge. can cream-style corn	

Place alternate layers of potatoes, onions, corn and sausage in a greased baking dish and cover with the tomato soup. Bake at 350 degrees for 1 hour.

Mrs. Cecil B. Howard, Maryville, Tennessee

BATTER-FRIED CHICKEN

1 3-lb. fryer, disjointed	1/4 tsp. pepper
2 c. flour	2 eggs
2 tsp. baking powder	3/4 c. milk
2 tsp. salt	1 1/2 tbsp. salad oil

Dredge the chicken with 1/2 cup flour. Sift the baking powder, salt, pepper and the remaining flour together into a bowl. Combine the eggs, milk and oil and beat with a rotary beater until blended, then add to the flour mixture. Beat until smooth. Dip the chicken into the batter, coating evenly. Fry in deep hot fat until golden brown. 4 servings.

Mrs. Billy M. Vaughan, Indian Mound, Tennessee

CHICKEN AND DUMPLINGS

1 4-lb. chicken with giblets	1 tsp. soda
1 qt. water	1 tsp. salt
4 c. sifted flour	1/2 c. shortening
2 tsp. baking powder	2 c. buttermilk

Cook the chicken and giblets in boiling salted water for 1 hour and 30 minutes or until tender. Drain and reserve the giblets and broth. Place the chicken in baking pan. Bake at 400 degrees until brown. Sift the flour, baking powder, soda and salt together in a bowl, then make a well in the flour mixture. Add the shortening and buttermilk and mix well, then knead 28 times. Roll out dough thin on floured board and cut into 2 x 5-inch strips. Bring the giblets and reserved broth to a rapid boil, then drop the dumplings in the boiling broth. Cover and cook for 18 minutes. Serve with the chicken. 6-8 servings.

Mrs. William E. Lake, St. Petersburg, Florida

KENTUCKY CHICKEN

2 c. fine bread crumbs	2 tsp. salt
3/4 c. grated Parmesan cheese	1/8 tsp. pepper
1 clove of garlic, crushed	1 3-lb. fryer, disjointed
(opt.)	1 c. melted butter
1/4 c. chopped parsley (opt.)	

Mix the bread crumbs, cheese, garlic, parsley, salt and pepper. Dip the chicken pieces into the butter, then into the crumb mixture, coating well. Arrange in a shallow pan, then pour the remaining butter over all. Bake at 350 degrees for 1 hour or until tender, basting frequently with the drippings. Do not turn chicken. 6 servings.

Mrs. Herschel Bennett, Irvington, Kentucky

SOUTHERN CHICKEN PIE

1 med. chicken	
5 tbsp. flour	2 hard-boiled eggs, chopped
Salt and pepper to taste	Diced pimentos to taste

Place the chicken in a saucepan and cover with boiling water. Cover the saucepan and simmer until chicken is tender. Cool chicken in broth. Remove chicken from broth. Remove skin and discard. Remove chicken from bones. Thicken broth with flour mixed with small amount of water and season with salt and pepper. Place chicken in a baking dish and add eggs and pimentos. Cover with broth.

Crust

1 c. flour	4 tbsp. shortening
1/2 tsp. salt	4 tbsp. cold water

Sift the flour with salt into a bowl and cut in shortening. Add the water, small amount at a time and mix well. Roll out on a floured surface and place on chicken mixture. Bake at 350 degrees for 30 to 45 minutes or until brown.

Mrs. Bill Bailey, Huntsville, Alabama

Vegetable-Chicken Supreme (below)

VEGETABLE-CHICKEN SUPREME

1 frying chicken, disjointed	2 tsp. paprika
1/4 lb. butter, melted	1 tsp. salt
3/4 c. fine dry bread crumbs	

Roll chicken in the butter. Combine the crumbs, paprika and salt and coat chicken pieces with the crumb mixture. Arrange pieces in a large shallow baking dish. Bake in 350-degree oven for 45 minutes.

Vegetables Supreme

1 1-lb. can cut Blue Lake green beans	1/4 tsp. salt
1 3-oz. can sliced mushrooms	1/4 c. fine dry bread crumbs
1 c. thinly sliced onion rings	1/8 tsp. garlic powder
2 tbsp. butter or margarine	1/8 tsp. pepper
	1/8 tsp. tarragon leaves
	1 c. sour cream

Drain the beans and the mushrooms, reserving mushroom liquid. Saute the mushrooms and onion in butter in large skillet until golden, then stir in the reserved liquid and remaining ingredients except the beans. Add the beans and heat through, tossing lightly. Serve with the chicken.

FRIED QUAIL

6 quail	Paprika
Salt and pepper to taste	Flour

Sprinkle the quail with salt, pepper and paprika, then dredge with flour. Fry in hot deep fat until golden brown. Serve immediately.

Mrs. Vann Hooker, Huttig, Arkansas

POTTED DOVE

6 dove	1 med. onion, quartered
Butter	4 sprigs of parsley
1 tbsp. flour	Salt and pepper to taste
2 c. chicken broth	

Rub the dove breasts with butter, then fry in hot fat until brown. Place dove in a casserole. Melt 2 tablespoons butter in a skillet, then blend in the flour until smooth. Add the broth gradually, stirring until smooth, then add the remaining ingredients except the dove. Simmer, stirring, until thickened. Pour the sauce over the dove. Bake, covered, at 325 degrees for 1 hour and 30 minutes. 6-8 servings.

Mrs. Owen Jones, Nashville, Tennessee

TURKEY IN FOIL

1 8 to 10-lb. turkey	1 c. water
Melted butter	

Preheat oven to 400 degrees. Place the turkey in center of large piece of foil and brush with butter. Pour water inside turkey and sew or skewer opening together. Bring foil up over the turkey, fold and seal. Place on rack in a roasting pan. Bake for 2 hours and 30 minutes to 3 hours. Open foil and bake for 45 minutes longer, basting occasionally with drippings in foil.

Mrs. Chester Hamilton, Mayfield, Kentucky

WILD DUCK WITH FRUIT

2 wild duck	Apple, orange and onion
Salt	quarters
1 tbsp. soda	4 slices bacon
Pepper	1/2 c. red Burgundy
Celery strips	Broiled button mushrooms

Place duck in a pan and cover with cold water. Add 1 tablespoon salt and soda and soak for 3 hours. Remove from water, rinse and drain thoroughly. Season each duck with salt and pepper and fill the cavities with celery, apple, orange and onion. Cover the breast of each duck with 2 slices bacon and place in a baking pan. Bake in 400-degree oven for 15 minutes. Cover and reduce temperature to 325 degrees. Bake for 15 minutes and add Burgundy. Cover and bake, basting frequently, for at least 3 hours. Remove breast bones and split each duck in half. Garnish with mushrooms.

Mrs. Mamie Tucker, Memphis, Tennessee

ASPARAGUS-CHEESE AND EGG CASSEROLE

2 tbsp. butter or margarine
2 tbsp. flour
1 2/3 c. evaporated milk
1/4 tsp. salt
1/4 tsp. pepper

2 c. cooked cut asparagus
3 hard-cooked eggs, sliced
8 thin slices cheese
1/4 c. chopped toasted almonds

Melt the butter in a saucepan, then stir in the flour until smooth. Add the milk gradually, stirring constantly. Cook over low heat, stirring, until thick and smooth. Season with salt and pepper. Arrange alternate layers of asparagus, eggs, cheese slices and almonds in a greased 1-quart casserole. Pour the sauce over casserole. Bake in a 350-degree oven for 20 minutes. 4-5 servings.

Mrs. Earl L. Faulkenberry, Lancaster, South Carolina

MUSHROOM-CHEESE SAUCE WITH GREEN BEANS

Butter
1/4 c. flour
1 tsp. salt
Dash of pepper
2 c. milk

1 c. shredded American cheese
1 c. sliced mushrooms
1 head cooked cauliflower
Cooked green beans

Melt the 1/4 cup butter in a saucepan over low heat, then blend in the flour, salt and pepper. Add the milk slowly and cook over low heat, stirring constantly, until sauce is smooth and thickened. Add the cheese, stirring until melted. Saute the mushrooms in 2 tablespoons butter until tender, then add to the hot sauce. Spoon over the cauliflower and green beans.

Mushroom-Cheese Sauce with Green Beans (above)
Minted-Glazed Carrots (page 102)

DOGPATCH TURNIPS

1 lb. turnips	1/3 c. cream
4 tbsp. butter, melted	Salt and pepper to taste
4 tbsp. flour	3 eggs, separated
1 tbsp. minced onion	

Wash, pare and slice the turnips, then place in a saucepan with 1 cup water and cook for 30 minutes or until soft. Drain, reserving 1/3 cup liquid, then mash. Combine the butter and flour in a saucepan, then add the onion, reserved liquid and cream gradually. Cook, stirring constantly, until thickened. Add the mashed turnips and seasonings, then stir in the well-beaten egg yolks. Fold in the stiffly beaten egg whites and pour into a buttered baking dish. Cover. Bake at 350 degrees until heated through. 6 servings.

Frances Moore, Kingfisher, Oklahoma

TURNIP GREENS WITH CORNMEAL DUMPLINGS

1 2-in. square salt pork	1/2 c. yellow cornmeal
1 bunch turnip greens	1/8 tsp. pepper
1/2 c. sifted flour	1 egg, lightly beaten
1 tsp. baking powder	1/4 c. milk
1/2 tsp. garlic salt	1 tbsp. melted butter

Slash the salt pork to the skin several times. Place in a large saucepan and add 3 inches water, then cook, covered, until tender. Wash and trim the greens and add to the pork. Cover and cook until tender, adding water if needed. Sift the dry ingredients into a mixing bowl, then add the egg, milk and butter, stirring until blended. Remove the greens and pork from the broth with a slotted spoon, then keep warm. Drop the dumplings by teaspoonfuls into the simmering broth. Cover tightly and simmer for 15 minutes. Do not lift cover. 4 servings.

Mrs. Thelma L. Fowler, Conce, Tennessee

SUMMER SQUASH

12 yellow squash, sliced	2 slices cooked bacon,
1 onion, grated	crumbled
4 tbsp. butter	Parmesan cheese to taste
Dash of Worcestershire sauce	2 eggs, well beaten
Salt and pepper to taste	Cracker crumbs
1/2 c. cream	

Cook the squash in water in a saucepan until tender. Drain well and mash. Cook the onion in butter in a saucepan until clear. Add the squash, Worcestershire sauce, salt, pepper, cream, bacon and cheese and stir over low heat until blended. Fold in the eggs. Pour into a greased casserole and cover with cracker crumbs. Dot with additional butter. Bake in 350-degree oven for 30 to 40 minutes. May be refrigerated for 24 hours before baking. 6-8 servings.

Mrs. E. Grady Covington, Howardsville, Virginia

CANDIED SWEET POTATOES

6 sweet potatoes, cooked	Pinch of salt
1 stick margarine, melted	2 tbsp. flour
1 c. sugar	1 3/4 c. orange juice

Peel and slice the sweet potatoes, then place in a baking dish. Combine the margarine, sugar, salt and flour in a saucepan and cook over low heat until the sugar is dissolved, stirring constantly. Add the orange juice and cook, stirring, until thickened. Pour over the potatoes. Bake at 350 degrees for 20 minutes. 10 servings.

Mrs. Bruce W. Sellers, Hamlet, North Carolina

GREEN LIMA BEANS

2 c. fresh green lima beans	1 tbsp. butter
3/4 c. water	1/2 tsp. sugar (opt.)
1 tsp. salt	1/3 c. heavy cream

Combine all the ingredients except cream in a saucepan and cook until the beans are tender. Add the cream and simmer for 5 minutes. Serve hot. 6-8 servings.

Mrs. Carol Murray, Murfreesboro, Tennessee

MINTED-GLAZED CARROTS

15 carrots, scraped	1/4 c. butter
1/4 c. honey	2 tsp. chopped mint leaves

Cook carrots in boiling salted water in a saucepan until tender, then drain. Add the honey and butter. Cook over low heat until carrots are glazed, turning several times. Sprinkle with mint just before serving. 4-6 servings.

Photograph for this recipe on page 100.

SOUTHERN-STYLE MUSTARD GREENS

Bacon	Salt and pepper to taste
Mustard greens	

Fry several slices of bacon in a heavy saucepan until crisp, then remove bacon. Add the greens to the drippings and cook, stirring frequently, until all the liquid has evaporated. Season with salt and pepper.

Gail Epperson, Slidell, Louisiana

EGGPLANT SUPREME

1 med. eggplant	1/2 tsp. pepper
1 1/2 c. milk	1 1/2 c. cracker crumbs
4 eggs, lightly beaten	1 1/2 c. grated cheese
1 tsp. salt	1 stick butter, melted

Peel and slice the eggplant, then place in a saucepan with 1 cup water. Cook until tender, then drain. Add the remaining ingredients except 1/2 cup crumbs, 1/2 cup cheese and a small amount of the melted butter. Mix well and pour into a baking dish, then sprinkle with the reserved crumbs, cheese and butter. Bake in 350-degree oven for about 25 to 30 minutes or until set. 4-6 servings.

Mrs. Mamie J. Caheely, Kensington, Georgia

HONEY-WHOLE WHEAT BREAD

1 c. milk, scalded	1 1/2 c. warm water
2 tbsp. sugar	3 1/2 c. sifted all-purpose
1 tsp. salt	flour
1/4 c. butter	4 c. unsifted whole wheat
1/2 c. honey or molasses	flour
2 pkg. dry yeast	Melted butter

Mix the milk, sugar, salt, butter and honey in a bowl and stir until butter is melted. Cool to lukewarm. Sprinkle yeast over warm water in a large bowl and stir until yeast is dissolved. Stir in the milk mixture. Add the flour and 2 1/2 cups whole wheat flour and beat until smooth. Add remaining whole wheat flour gradually and mix until dough leaves side of bowl. Turn out onto a lightly floured board and cover with a bowl. Let rest for 10 minutes. Knead for about 10 minutes or until smooth and elastic. Place in a lightly greased bowl and turn to grease top. Cover with a towel and let rise in a warm place, free from draft, for about 1 hour and 15 minutes or until doubled in bulk. Punch down. Turn out onto a floured pastry cloth and divide in half. Shape each half into smooth ball. Cover with a towel and let rest for 10 minutes. Shape each ball into a loaf and place in 2 greased loaf pans. Brush with melted butter. Cover with a towel and let rise until dough reaches top of pans. Bake at 400 degrees for 50 minutes.

Mrs. F. C. Abraham, Tracy City, Tennessee

KENTUCKY BEATEN BISCUITS

4 c. sifted flour	1 c. lard or vegetable
1 tsp. salt	shortening
2 tbsp. sugar	1 c. cold milk
1 tsp. baking powder	1/4 c. ice water

Sift the flour, salt, sugar and baking powder together in a mixing bowl, then cut in lard until of meal consistency. Mix the milk and water together, then pour all at once into flour mixture, stirring to make a stiff dough. Turn out onto a floured board and knead for about 5 minutes. Roll through a biscuit kneader, folding each time, for about 25 times or until dough pops and is soft and velvety. Keep well floured with additional flour to prevent sticking. Roll out 1/4 to 1/2 inch thick, then cut with small biscuit cutter. Place on a baking sheet. Prick through the dough with a fork. Bake at 350 degrees for about 40 minutes. Dough may be beaten with heavy rolling pin and worked to smooth waxy consistency that pops if biscuit kneader is not available.

Mrs. Kenneth V. O'Neal, Lexington, Kentucky

Blueberry Corn Bread (below)

BLUEBERRY CORN BREAD

1 c. fresh blueberries	4 tsp. baking powder
1 1/2 c. flour	2 eggs, beaten
1 c. yellow cornmeal	2 c. milk
1/4 c. sugar	1/4 c. shortening, melted
1/2 tsp. salt	

Wash the blueberries and drain well in a colander or on paper towels. Sift the flour, cornmeal, sugar, salt and baking powder into a bowl. Mix the eggs, milk and shortening, then add to the dry ingredients and beat until smooth. Fold in blueberries carefully. Preheat an electric skillet for 5 minutes at 250 degrees and grease. Pour the batter into skillet. Bake, covered, with vent open for 25 to 30 minutes. Serve hot from skillet at breakfast table. May be baked in a well-greased pan in 425-degree preheated oven for 30 minutes, if desired.

COLONIAL WHITE BREAD

2 tbsp. sugar	1 1/2 c. warm water
2 tsp. salt	1 pkg. yeast
3 tbsp. butter or shortening	5 1/2 c. (about) flour
1/2 c. milk, scalded	

Stir the sugar, salt and butter into the milk, then cool to lukewarm. Pour the warm water into large warm bowl, then sprinkle in the yeast, stirring until dissolved. Add the lukewarm milk mixture and 3 cups flour and beat until smooth. Add enough remaining flour to make a soft dough. Turn out onto lightly floured board. Knead for about 8 to 10 minutes or until smooth and elastic. Form into a smooth ball and place in a greased bowl, turning to grease the top. Cover and let rise in a warm place, free from drafts, for about 1 hour or until doubled in bulk. Punch down and let rest for 15 minutes. Divide dough in half, then shape each half into a loaf. Place in greased 9 x 5 x 3-inch bread pans. Cover let rise in a warm place, free from drafts, for about 1 hour or until doubled in bulk. Bake at 400 degrees for about 30 minutes.

Mrs. Allie M. Stauffer, Kellysville, West Virginia

SETTLER'S BREAD

1/2 c. cornmeal	1 tsp. salt
2 c. boiling water	1 pkg. yeast
2 tbsp. shortening	1/2 c. warm water
1/2 c. molasses	6 c. flour

Stir the cornmeal slowly into the boiling water and mix well. Stir in the shortening, molasses and salt and cool to lukewarm. Dissolve the yeast in the warm water, then stir into the cornmeal mixture. Add the flour, then knead until smooth. Place in a large greased bowl in a warm place. Cover and let rise until doubled in bulk. Turn out onto floured board and divide in half. Punch down and shape each half into a loaf. Place in a greased bread pan and let rise until doubled in bulk. Bake at 375 degrees for 1 hour.

Mrs. Inez Robbins, Phenix City, Alabama

SOURDOUGH BISCUITS WITH STARTER

1 c. whole-wheat flour	1 tsp. baking powder
1 c. all-purpose flour	1/2 c. butter
1 tbsp. sugar	2 c. Starter
1 tsp. salt	

Combine the first 5 ingredients in a bowl, then cut in the butter with a pastry blender until mixture resembles coarse crumbs. Stir in the Starter. Turn the dough onto a floured board and knead lightly. Roll 1/2 inch thick and cut in 2 1/2-inch circles. Place on a lightly greased cookie sheet. Let rise in a warm place for 30 minutes. Bake at 425 degrees for 20 to 25 minutes or until lightly browned.

Starter

1 env. dry yeast	2 c. all-purpose flour
2 c. warm water	

Combine all the ingredients in 1 1/2-quart glass or earthenware container and mix well. Cover with cheesecloth. Let stand at room temperature for 48 hours, stirring 2 or 3 times. Starter will ferment and acquire slightly sour smell. Pour off as much Starter as recipe requires, then add equal parts water and flour to starter. Let stand for several hours until bubbly again. Refrigerate.

Lydia Lee Byrd, Norman, Oklahoma

GLAZED RAISIN LOAF

1 c. seedless raisins	1 pkg. yeast
1/4 c. soft butter	1/4 c. lukewarm water
1/4 c. sugar	2 eggs, well beaten
1 tsp. salt	4 c. sifted flour
1/2 c. scalded milk	

Combine the raisins, butter, sugar, salt and milk in a mixing bowl and cool to lukewarm. Dissolve the yeast in lukewarm water. Add yeast, eggs and 1 cup flour to raisin mixture and beat until smooth. Add remaining flour gradually and beat until well mixed. Cover and let rest for 10 minutes. Knead on a lightly floured surface until smooth and elastic. Place in a greased bowl and turn to grease surface. Cover and let rise in a warm place until doubled in bulk. Punch down and let rest for 10 minutes. Shape into a loaf and place in a greased 9 x 5 x 3-inch loaf pan. Cover and let rise until almost doubled in bulk. Bake at 375 degrees for about 50 minutes or until brown. Cool and glaze with thin powdered sugar icing, if desired.

Glennette Kay Kaiser, Moulton, Texas

RAISIN KULITCH

1 c. scalded milk, cooled	1/2 tsp. salt
1 pkg. yeast	1 c. mixed dark and light raisins
Sugar	1/4 c. chopped citron
4 1/2 c. (about) flour	1/2 c. chopped candied orange peel
1/2 c. margarine	1 tsp. grated lemon peel
2 eggs, beaten	1 c. chopped nuts

Combine the milk, yeast, 1 tablespoon sugar and 1/2 cup flour in a bowl and mix well. Let stand for 45 minutes. Cream the margarine and 1/2 cup sugar in a bowl and stir in the yeast mixture. Add eggs and mix well. Add salt and enough flour for stiff dough and mix well. Stir in remaining ingredients. Knead on a floured surface until smooth and elastic. Place in 2 greased 3-pound shortening cans and let rise until dough is nearly to top of cans. Bake at 400 degrees for 15 minutes. Reduce temperature to 350 degrees and bake for 30 to 45 minutes longer. Cool in cans for 10 minutes. Remove from cans and cool on rack.

Mrs. Fletcher Thompson, Clarksville, Arkansas

WALNUT COFFEE CAKE

1/2 c. butter or margarine	1 1/2 tsp. baking powder
1 1/2 c. sugar	1 tsp. soda
2 eggs	1/4 tsp. salt
1 tsp. vanilla	1 c. chopped walnuts
1 c. sour cream	1 tsp. cinnamon
2 c. sifted flour	1 1/2 c. seedless raisins

Cream the butter and 1 cup sugar in a bowl until fluffy. Add the eggs and vanilla and beat well. Blend in the sour cream. Sift the flour, baking powder, soda and salt together and stir into creamed mixture. Spread half the batter in a greased 9-inch square pan. Mix the walnuts, remaining sugar and cinnamon and sprinkle half the mixture over batter. Sprinkle with raisins. Add remaining batter and top with remaining walnut mixture. Bake at 350 degrees for 40 minutes. Cut into squares and serve warm. 9 servings.

Mrs. Danny Duckworth, Morganton, North Carolina

BLACKBERRY JAM PIE

8 eggs	1 c. blackberry jam
3 c. sugar	2 unbaked 9-in. pie shells
1 o. moltod margarine	

Beat the eggs well, then add the sugar and margarine. Mix until well blended. Beat in the jam and pour into the pie shells. Bake at 400 degrees for 10 minutes. Reduce the oven temperature to 350 degrees and bake until a knife inserted in center comes out clean.

Kathryn Smith, Jayton, Texas

CHESTNUT PUREE WITH CREAM

1 1/2 lb. chestnuts	1/2 pt. heavy cream, whipped
1 c. sugar	Nutmeg
1/2 c. rum	

Shell and skin the chestnuts. Place in a saucepan and cover with boiling water. Add the sugar and cook until chestnuts are soft. Drain and mash. Add rum and chill. Serve with whipped cream and sprinkle with nutmeg. 6 servings.

Mrs. Henry Church, Chattanooga, Tennessee

OLD-FASHIONED POUND CAKE

2 sticks butter	3 c. flour
2 c. sugar	1/4 tsp. salt
6 eggs	1 tbsp. vanilla

Cream the butter and sugar together in a mixing bowl. Add the eggs, one at a time, beating well after each addition. Mix the flour and salt together, then add to the creamed mixture, a small amount at a time, beating well after each addition. Stir in the vanilla. Place in a greased tube or loaf pan. Bake at 350 degrees for 1 hour or until cake tests done.

Mrs. George Collins, Greeneville, Tennessee

Christmas Pudding (below)

CHRISTMAS PUDDING

2 3/4 c. bread crumbs
1 c. diced California dried
  figs
1 1/2 c. seedless raisins
3/4 c. mixed candied fruit
1/2 c. dried currants
1/2 c. toasted filberts,
  chopped
2 c. ground suet
1 1/2 tsp. salt
3/4 tsp. cinnamon

1/2 tsp. mace
1/4 tsp. cloves
1 c. scalded milk
1/2 c. (packed) dark brown
  sugar
4 eggs
2 tbsp. brandy
2 tbsp. orange juice or red
  wine
Brandied Figs

Grease a 2-quart mold and coat with 3 to 4 tablespoons of the bread crumbs. Combine the fruits, filberts and suet in a large bowl. Mix the remaining bread crumbs, salt, spices, milk and brown sugar in a large bowl and stir until the sugar dissolves. Add the eggs, brandy and juice and beat until well blended. Stir in the fruit mixture. Pour into the prepared mold and cover tightly. Place mold on rack in bottom of large pot or roaster and fill with enough boiling water to cover 2/3 of the mold. Cover and steam pudding for 5 hours, adding water as needed. Pour off any excess fat from top of pudding. Cool for about 1 hour before unmolding. Garnish with Brandied Figs. Serve warm with lemon or hard sauce. Pudding may be made ahead and reheated in mold before serving.

Brandied Figs

2/3 c. sugar
30 California dried figs

1/2 c. cognac

Combine 2 cups water and sugar in a large saucepan, then bring to a boil, stirring until sugar dissolves. Add the figs and cover, then simmer for 15 minutes. Add the cognac and cook for 5 minutes longer or until figs are plump and soft. Cool, then turn into bowl and chill for 24 hours or longer. Serve with cream.

WOODFORD PUDDING

1/2 c. butter	1 1/2 c. sifted flour
1 c. sugar	1/2 tsp. cinnamon
3 eggs	1/2 tsp. nutmeg
1 c. blackberry jam	1/2 c. chopped nuts
1 tsp. soda	1/2 c. raisins
3 tbsp. buttermilk	

Cream the butter and sugar in a bowl and stir in the eggs and jam. Dissolve the soda in buttermilk and stir into creamed mixture. Sift the flour with cinnamon and nutmeg and stir into creamed mixture. Add the nuts and raisins and mix well. Pour into a greased 9-inch square pan. Bake at 325 degrees for about 45 minutes or until pudding tests done. Cut in squares.

Butterscotch Sauce

1 1/2 c. (packed) brown sugar	2 tbsp. butter
4 tbsp. flour	2 tbsp. cream
1 c. boiling water	Vanilla to taste
Dash of salt	

Mix the brown sugar with flour in a saucepan. Add the water and salt and blend well. Cook, stirring, for 6 to 8 minutes or until thick, adding water, if needed. Remove from heat and stir in butter, cream and vanilla. Pour over pudding.

Mrs. James Morrison, Campbellsville, Kentucky

KENTUCKY MINT JULEP CAKE

2 1/2 c. sifted flour	1 tbsp. creme de menthe
1 1/2 c. sugar	3 egg whites
3 tsp. baking powder	1/2 c. butter
1 tsp. salt	1 lb. confectioners' sugar
1/2 c. margarine, softened	2 tbsp. cream
1 c. milk	1/2 tsp. almond flavoring

Preheat the oven to 350 degrees. Sift the first 4 ingredients together in a mixing bowl, then add the margarine, 3/4 cup milk and creme de menthe. Beat until flour is moistened. Add the egg whites and remaining milk and beat until smooth. Spoon batter into 2 greased 9-inch layer pans. Bake for 25 minutes or until cake tests done. Cool. Blend the remaining ingredients together until of spreading consistency, then frost the cake. Decorate cake with fresh mint sprigs, if desired.

Mrs. Robert E. Gillis, Louisville, Kentucky

STACK CAKE

3 c. flour	1/2 c. shortening
1/2 tsp. soda	1/2 c. buttermilk
1/2 tsp. salt	1 tsp. vanilla
1/2 tsp. baking powder	2 c. cooked dried fruit,
3/4 c. sugar	drained

Sift the dry ingredients together, then knead in the shortening. Add the buttermilk and vanilla and mix well. Divide into 6 equal parts and roll thin. Fit each part into a 9-inch cake pan. Prick with a fork. Bake at 475 degrees for 5 to 10 minutes or until medium brown. Cool. Mash the fruit and sweeten to taste with additional sugar. Spread the fruit between the layers. Apples, peaches or apricots may be used, adding 1/2 teaspoon nutmeg or cinnamon if apples are used. 10 servings.

Anna Lee Stubblefield, Greenville, Tennessee

DUTCH APPLE PUDDING CAKE

1 pkg. yellow cake mix	1 1/2 c. apple juice
1 c. milk	1/2 tsp. cinnamon
1 c. chopped walnuts	1/2 tsp. allspice
2 7 3/4-oz. jars junior baby	1/4 tsp. nutmeg
food Dutch apple dessert	

Blend the cake mix with the milk until moistened, then stir in the walnuts. Spread in a greased 3-quart shallow baking dish. Combine the baby food, apple juice and spices in a saucepan and stir until mixture comes to a boil. Pour over the cake batter. Bake in a 350-degree oven for about 1 hour. Serve warm with cream.

Dutch Apple Pudding Cake (above)

WHISKEY CAKE

1 lb. red candied cherries	6 eggs, separated
1/2 lb. golden raisins	5 c. sifted flour
2 c. whiskey	2 tsp. nutmeg
3/4 lb. butter	1 tsp. baking powder
2 c. sugar	4 c. pecan halves
1 c. (packed) brown sugar	

Cut the cherries in half into a bowl, then add the raisins and whiskey and soak overnight. Cream butter and sugars together in a mixing bowl until fluffy, then add the egg yolks, one at a time, beating well after each addition. Add the fruit mixture and flour, mixing well. Add the nutmeg and baking powder. Fold in the stiffly beaten egg whites. Stir in the pecans. Turn into a large greased tube pan lined with greased paper. Bake at 250 degrees for 3 hours or until cake tests done. Cool. May stuff center hole with cheesecloth soaked in additional whiskey, if desired. Wrap in heavy waxed paper. Store in covered container in refrigerator or freezer. 24 servings.

Mrs. Rose Dale, Williamsburg, Kentucky

DELUXE BLACKBERRY COBBLER

1 c. flour	3/4 c. milk
1 c. sugar	1 stick butter, melted
1/4 tsp. salt	2 1/2 c. blackberries,
2 tsp. baking powder	sweetened

Mix the dry ingredients together in a baking dish, then stir in the milk. Pour the melted butter over the dough and spoon the blackberries on top. Bake at 350 degrees for 45 minutes or until dough rises to top and browns. 6-8 servings.

Mrs. Christel Bullard, Zwolle, Louisiana

KENTUCKY BOURBON BALLS

1/2 c. finely chopped nuts	1 1-lb. box confectioners'
1/2 c. finely chopped	sugar
candied cherries	2 8-oz. boxes semisweet
1/2 c. bourbon	chocolate
1 stick butter or margarine	1 box paraffin

Combine the nuts and cherries in a bowl and stir in bourbon. Let stand for 2 to 3 hours and drain well. Cream the butter and sugar in a bowl and add nuts and cherries. Shape in small balls and refrigerate for 30 minutes. Melt the chocolate and paraffin in top of a double boiler over hot water. Dip bourbon balls in melted chocolate mixture and place on waxed paper. Cool. 2 dozen.

Mrs. Melba Garrett, Decatur, Georgia

favorite foods of georgia

By the time the first colonists had begun to settle coastal Georgia and explorers were infiltrating the western piedmont, Deep South cuisine had been developing for more than one hundred years. If it was not well defined as it is today, it was sufficiently established to have an almost immediate effect on recipes the newcomers brought to Georgia. Perhaps that is why this section on the foods of Georgia features so many of the South's most traditional dishes.

One such dish is South Georgia Squirrel Stew, a recipe closely related to the Brunswick stew recipes found throughout the Deep South. Another typically southern recipe is Hoe Cakes. Originally this cornbread derived its name because it was baked on a hoe handle in the hot coals of the family's fireplace. Despite the introduction of modern stoves and pans and the disappearance of hoe handles and fireplaces as cooking equipment, the name and its hint of a colorful past remain. Stewed Okra and Tomatoes is still another recipe that is important to Deep South cookery. Okra is not native to the region but was brought by African slaves who found that it thrived here.

As you browse through these pages, you'll discover many other dishes that are essential components of what we know as Deep South cookery. Treat your family to some of them tonight — they're all home-tested, so you can be certain of delicious dining.

Of all the Deep South's Atlantic colonies, Georgia was the last to be formally settled. Beginning in the late 1600's, enterprising settlers and trappers traveled the length of the Shenandoah Valley, coming out onto a piedmont and then followed a river that led to the site of present-day Augusta. However, few of these explorers stayed: this region was not only Indian territory, it was also claimed by the Spanish who periodically established forts and trading posts to discourage would-be settlers.

In 1732, undaunted by the dual threat of Spaniards and Indians, England's King George awarded General James Oglethorpe, an English member of Parliament, all the land lying between the Savannah and Altamaha rivers. This

HISTORY AND TRADITIONS OF

land granting was followed by the most prodigious publicity campaign of any potential colonization of the New World. Posters and handbills were distributed throughout England and parts of Europe, citing the virtues of the new colony and inviting potential colonists to contact General Oglethorpe.

The General was interested in colonizing the new land for two reasons. First, as an army man, he appreciated the need to establish a buffer zone between the hostile territory of Spanish Florida and the flourishing English colonies in the Carolinas and Virginia. Second, he was also a humanitarian who had been much moved by the plight of his fellow Englishmen trapped in debtors' prisons. He forsaw that many of these debtors could get a fresh start in a new colony. But he was wise enough to know that humanitarian instincts were not enough — the first shipload of settlers contained not only debtors but consisted of farmers, a surgeon, a druggist, and several artisans or tradesmen — including two makers of men's wigs! This mixed group landed at the site of present day Savannah in spring of 1733.

The new colony was profitable for most of the settlers. Many stayed in the coastal lowlands where they grew cotton, tobacco, indigo, and rice. As these crops thrived, the plantation owners moved out of their small wooden cabins into magnificent mansions built on Greek revival or Georgian lines. Here, as elsewhere in the South, hospitality was the rule. An Englishman traveling in Georgia about twenty years after the first settlements had been made, recorded that one plantation owner "received and entertained me in every respect, as a worthy gentleman could a stranger, that is, with hearty welcome, plain but plentiful board, free conversation and liberality of sentiment."

Certainly the settlers of Georgia had developed a reputation of hospitality equal to that of any older, longer-established colony.

The "plain but plentiful" food was typical of the cuisine of many early Georgian homes. Fish abounded in the waters of the region, and nearly every farm or plantation was located on a river or its tributaries. Along the coast, shellfish were plentiful. Foods such as hot breads and biscuits together with rice — always available in the lowlands where rice was a staple crop — were served often. Vegetables fresh from the garden would be accompanied by homemade preserves of locally grown produce. Ham or chicken were the main dishes. To finish the meal, proud Georgian homemakers often served a cake, pie, or other sweet and rich dessert. One favorite was pound cake, so called because it used a pound of butter, a pound of sugar, and a pound of eggs, among other ingredients.

Once a traveler moved away from the lowland settlements, he encountered a rapid change in the countryside. Palmettos gave way to pine trees; the sandy loam of the coast was replaced by the red clay of the Piedmont; and the large plantation tended to be replaced by smaller, family-operated farms. Here, as in the coastal settlements, hospitality reigned. Every stranger was welcomed as a source of news from the outside world. As he shared his news, the family shared its food with him. That food differed from what was served in the coastal lowlands. Corn bread appeared on the tables and rice was seldom seen. Frequently, dairy products such as milk, cream, butter, and cheese from the family's herd were served. In the uplands as along the coast, ham and chicken were staple foods, but far more prominent were venison and small game as well as the ever-present local version of Brunswick Stew.

In the years between the first settlement of Georgia and the American Revolution, other influences appeared in the region, altering aspects of the people's lives — including the foods they ate. For example, many French Huguenots arrived from France or from South Carolina and found the city of Savannah to their liking. To this day, the foods served in Savannah have a distinctly French style. German emigrants settled further up the Savannah River at a site they named Ebenezer. The cookery of this region is made up in part of sauerkraut, pepper pot soup, and other distinctively German dishes. Some Scots Highland clans or families, seeking independence from England, found their freedom along the Altamaha River where they built the city of Frederica. The foods on their tables echoed the dishes served in their native Highlands.

So it came to be that Georgia's cuisine, like that of most of the Deep South, was a combination of that which was past and that which is present. The cuisine had its roots in the Old World that provided memories and recipes frontier women used to prepare the foods they found in the New World. As elsewhere in the Deep South, the foods of Georgia emerged as something unique to that section.

CHICKEN-PEANUT STEW

1 2 1/2 to 3-lb. chicken	1 c. finely chopped parched
Salt and pepper to taste	peanuts
1 pt. crunchy peanut butter	Cooked rice

Place the chicken in a saucepan and add 1 1/2 quarts boiling water. Add the salt and pepper and simmer until tender. Drain and reserve broth. Cool chicken and remove chicken from bones. Remove skin and discard. Cut chicken in small pieces. Add 1 cup reserved broth to peanut butter gradually and stir until smooth. Stir into remaining broth in the saucepan and blend until smooth. Add chicken and peanuts and mix well. Heat through. Serve on rice with accompaniments of riced hard-boiled eggs, chopped onion, chopped green pepper, diced celery, red hot pepper, diced cucumbers, grated coconut and grated carrots.

Mrs. R. Darnell, Morristown, Tennessee

CHICKEN SOUP WITH MILK

1 broiler	1 biscuit
Salt and pepper to taste	Butter
2 c. milk	

Place the chicken in a saucepan and cover with water. Bring to a boil and reduce heat. Simmer until chicken is tender. Remove chicken from broth and cool. Remove chicken from bones and cut in small pieces. Add to broth and season with salt and pepper. Pour in milk and bring to a boil. Split the biscuit and spread with butter. Toast until brown, then crumble into soup.

Mrs. J. Carlton Tyler, Monticello, Georgia

PEACH SOUP

1 pt. water	2 c. sliced peaches
1/8 tsp. cinnamon	2 c. white wine
2 whole cloves	Sugar to taste

Combine the water, spices and peaches in a saucepan and simmer until the peaches are tender. Press through a colander. Stir in the wine and sugar and heat just to boiling point. Chill. Serve in bouillon cups. Apple cider or grape juice may be substituted for wine. 6 servings.

Mrs. Irby J. Hornsby, Montegut, Louisiana

SOUTH GEORGIA SQUIRREL STEW

2 squirrels	2 c. lima beans
1 gal. water	3 c. canned tomatoes
2 tsp. salt	2 c. diced carrots
1/2 tsp. pepper	5 potatoes, diced
2 lge. onions, sliced	4 c. corn
2 c. sliced okra	6 tbsp. butter

Cut the squirrels into serving pieces. Bring the water to a boil in a kettle and add the squirrels, 1 piece at a time. Add the salt, pepper, onions, okra, lima beans, tomatoes, carrots and potatoes and bring to a boil. Reduce heat and simmer for 4 hours, adding water as needed. Add the corn and simmer for 1 hour longer, stirring occasionally. Add the butter just before serving. 6 servings.

Mrs. Sarah Thompson, Dam Neck, Virginia

SHRIMP SALAD

2 c. cleaned cooked shrimp	1/4 c. chili sauce
1/2 c. sliced celery	3 tbsp. fresh lemon juice
1 tsp. minced onion	2 hard-cooked eggs, chopped
1/3 c. mayonnaise	Salt and pepper to taste

Combine all the ingredients and mix well. Chill thoroughly, then serve on lettuce. 6 servings.

Frances B. Kniceley, Winchester, Virginia

PEACHY BLUE CHEESE SALAD

1 1-lb. can cling peach slices	1/2 c. salad dressing
1 pkg. peach gelatin	1/4 c. chopped celery
1 5-oz. jar blue cheese spread	2 or 3 tbsp. ripe olive wedges
	Salad greens

Drain the syrup from peaches and add enough water, if needed, to make 1 cup liquid. Pour into a saucepan and bring to a boil. Add the gelatin and stir until dissolved. Blend in the cheese spread and salad dressing and chill until partially set. Mix in the celery, olives and peaches, reserving several peach slices for garnish. Pour into a 1-quart mold and chill until firm. Unmold and garnish with peach slices and crisp salad greens. 6 servings.

Peachy Blue Cheese Salad (above)

CHEESE-CUCUMBER SALAD

1 3-oz. package lime gelatin	1 carton cottage cheese
1/2 c. hot water	1 c. mayonnaise
3/4 c. grated cucumber	1/2 c. slivered almonds
2 tbsp. grated onion	Dash of salt

Dissolve the gelatin in hot water. Add remaining ingredients and mix well. Pour into a mold and chill until firm.

Mrs. Sinclair G. Stewart, Atlanta, Georgia

FRESH PEACH SALAD

8 fresh peeled peaches, sliced	1 c. sour cream
1/4 c. sugar	1 tbsp. mayonnaise

Place the peaches in a bowl. Mix the sugar, sour cream and mayonnaise and pour over peaches. Mix well and chill thoroughly. Serve on lettuce leaves. 6 servings.

Mrs. Crystal E. Durant, Pensacola, Florida

PEACHY HAM BALLS

1 lb. ground cooked ham	1/8 tsp. ground cloves
1/3 c. fine dry bread crumbs	8 canned cling peach halves
2/3 c. evaporated milk	1 tbsp. prepared mustard
Brown sugar	

Combine the ground ham, bread crumbs, evaporated milk, 1 tablespoon brown sugar and cloves and shape into 8 balls. Drain the peach halves and reserve 1/4 cup syrup. Place 8 peach halves, cut side up, in a shallow, buttered baking dish and fill hollow of each half with a ham ball. Combine 1/2 cup packed brown sugar, mustard and reserved peach syrup and pour over ham balls. Bake in 350-degree oven for 15 minutes. Baste the ham balls with liquid in pan and bake for 15 minutes longer.

Peachy Ham Balls (above)

CHEESE AND BLACK WALNUT SALAD

1 8-oz. package cream cheese	1 1/3 c. finely chopped black walnuts
Cream	Lettuce
Salt and pepper to taste	Mayonnaise

Mash the cream cheese and stir in enough cream to moisten. Season with salt and pepper. Stir in the walnuts and shape into small balls. Arrange on lettuce and serve with mayonnaise.

Dena G. Owen, Decatur, Georgia

SHRIMP-CURRY SALAD

1 1 1/2-lb. bag frozen	1/2 c. chutney
cleaned shrimp	1 1/2 tsp. salt
3 c. cooked rice	3/4 c. French dressing
2 c. cooked peas	1/2 to 1 tsp. curry powder
2 c. diced celery	

Prepare the shrimp according to package directions, then place in a bowl and chill. Add remaining ingredients and toss well. Chill. Serve on salad greens. 6 servings.

Mrs. Virginia F. Sheppard, Camilla, Georgia

PICKLED PEACHES

1 c. sugar	3 qt. Indian peaches,
1 c. vinegar	peeled
1 c. water	Cloves

Combine the sugar, vinegar and water in a saucepan and bring to boiling point, stirring frequently. Stud each peach with 2 cloves and add to the syrup. Cook until peaches are tender. Pack the peaches in sterilized jars and cover with syrup. Seal.

Mrs. C. T. Spigner, Foreman, Arkansas

CHICKEN-FRIED STEAK

1/2 c. flour	3 tbsp. shortening
2 tsp. salt	1/2 c. hot water
1/8 tsp. pepper	1/2 c. cream
2 lb. round steak	

Mix the flour, salt and pepper and pound into the steak. Brown steak on both sides in hot shortening in a skillet. Add the water and cream and cover. Simmer until steak is tender.

Cora Pearl Stogner, Shadpoint, Oklahoma

BEEF A LA MODE

1 6-lb. beef round or chuck	Vinegar
1/2 lb. sliced bacon, cut in sm. pieces	Salt and pepper to taste
	Shortening
3 med. onions, chopped	Flour
Whole cloves	1 bay leaf

Cut deep gashes into the beef with a sharp knife and stuff gashes with bacon, onions and cloves. Bind with cord to keep in seasonings, if necessary. Place in a large, deep bowl and fill bowl with equal parts of vinegar and water. Refrigerate for 12 hours, turning the beef occasionally. Remove beef from vinegar mixture and season with salt and pepper. Rub with shortening and coat with flour. Cook in small amount of shortening in a Dutch oven over high heat until brown on all sides. Pour the vinegar mixture into the Dutch oven and add bay leaf. Cover. Cook over low heat for about 6 hours, turning beef occasionally and adding water, if needed. Pour off excess fat and thicken gravy.

Mrs. David S. Hanson, Augusta, Georgia

GEORGIA BEEF PIE

3 tbsp. fat	1/4 tsp. pepper
3 tbsp. flour	2 c. diced cooked beef
1 1/2 c. meat stock or bouillon	1 c. cooked peas
1 1/2 tsp. salt	2 c. seasoned mashed potatoes

Melt the fat in a saucepan and blend in flour. Add the meat stock and cook, stirring constantly, until thickened. Season with salt and pepper. Add the beef and peas and pour into a casserole. Spoon potatoes around the edge of casserole. Bake in 425-degree oven for about 15 minutes or until potatoes are browned. 4-6 servings.

M. V. Tracy, Coyle, Oklahoma

BAKED HAM WITH PEACHES

1 slice ham	Peach halves
1/2 c. (packed) brown sugar	Melted butter
2 tbsp. vinegar	Crushed corn flakes
1/2 tsp. mustard	Currant jelly

Place the ham in a baking pan. Bake in 375-degree oven until fat browns. Mix the brown sugar, vinegar and mustard and spread over ham. Cover the baking pan. Decrease temperature to 300 degrees and bake for 1 hour and 30 minutes longer. Brush the peach halves with butter and roll in corn flake crumbs. Place in a baking dish. Bake at 450 degrees until brown. Place 1 teaspoon currant jelly in cavity of each peach and arrange peach halves around ham.

Mrs. Edith Shore, East Bend, North Carolina

TALMADGE COUNTRY-FRIED HAM

1 slice country ham,	1 c. buttermilk
1/4 in. thick	3 tbsp. brown sugar

Trim off skin from ham, leaving as much fat as possible. Score the fat and place in a shallow pan. Mix the buttermilk and sugar and pour over the ham. Soak for 30 minutes. Place ham in a hot, greased skillet and brown on both sides over medium heat. Place on a platter. Add 1 cup water to drippings in skillet and simmer until liquid is reduced by half. Serve with ham. Ham may be soaked in warm water for 15 minutes instead of in buttermilk.

Mrs. Herman E. Talmadge, Lovejoy, Georgia

ROAST LOIN OF PORK

1 4-lb. pork loin roast	Oil
2 lge. Spanish onions, quartered	Salt and pepper to taste
4 lge. potatoes, halved	Powdered sage to taste

Place the pork roast in a shallow baking pan and place onions and potatoes around roast. Brush the vegetables with oil and sprinkle with salt, pepper and sage. Bake at 325 degrees for 2 hours, basting vegetables with pan drippings every 30 minutes.

Mrs. Everette M. Waters, Dallas, Georgia

BRAISED RABBIT

1 frying rabbit	2 2-oz. cans mushrooms
Seasoned flour	Salt to taste
1 lge. can evaporated milk	

Cut the rabbit into serving pieces and dredge with seasoned flour. Brown in small amount of hot fat in a skillet, then place in a roasting pan. Add the milk, mushrooms and salt. Bake at 350 degrees for 1 hour or until rabbit is well done.

Mrs. L. P. Montgomery, Pollock, Louisiana

QUICK SAUSAGE AND GRITS DELIGHT

1/2 lb. link sausage	1 c. quick-cooking grits
4 c. water	Pancake mix
1 tsp. salt	

Brown the link sausage in a skillet over high heat, then cut into 1/4-inch thick slices. Reserve 1 tablespoon drippings. Pour the water into a saucepan and bring to a boil. Add the salt, reserved drippings and sausage. Stir in the grits and cook over medium heat for 3 minutes. Pour into a loaf pan and chill. Cut the grits into 1/2-inch slices and dredge with pancake mix. Brown in small amount of fat in a skillet, then drain on absorbent paper.

Henrietta Fuller, Atlanta, Georgia

CONFEDERATE CHICKEN

1 3 1/2-lb. chicken	1 tbsp. flour
1/4 c. chopped onion	1 lge. can tomatoes
3 cloves of garlic, chopped	1 tsp. salt
5 tbsp. chopped green pepper	Pepper to taste
1 tsp. parsley flakes	1 bay leaf
2 tsp. butter	1/2 c. white wine

Cut the chicken into serving pieces. Brown in a small amount of fat in a skillet, then remove from skillet. Saute the onion, garlic, green pepper and parsley in remaining fat in the skillet until tender. Add the butter and flour and cook, stirring, until brown. Stir in remaining ingredients. Add the chicken and cover. Simmer for 1 hour and 30 minutes, stirring occasionally and adding water, if needed.

Mrs. Allen Mayes, Cartersville, Georgia

GRANDMA'S CHICKEN PIE

1 5-lb. hen	1/2 tsp. salt
3 stalks celery and leaves	Dash of pepper
3 tbsp. flour	1 c. milk
3 tbsp. melted butter	

Place the hen and celery in a kettle and cover with boiling water. Cook until chicken is tender. Drain and reserve 3 cups broth. Cool the chicken. Remove the skin and grind. Remove chicken from bones and cut in bite-sized pieces. Mix with ground skin and place in a greased baking pan. Add the flour to butter in a saucepan and stir well. Add the salt, pepper, reserved broth and milk and cook until thickened, stirring constantly. Pour over chicken.

Crust

2 c. flour	1 egg, well beaten
2 tsp. baking powder	2 tbsp. chicken fat or butter
1 tsp. salt	1 c. milk

Sift the flour, baking powder and salt into a bowl. Add the egg, fat and milk and mix well. Drop by spoonfuls on chicken mixture. Bake at 400 degrees for 40 minutes or until brown.

Mrs. C. Howard Evans, West Palm Beach, Florida

BANQUET BROILERS

6 sm. broilers	3 boxes long grain and wild
Salt and pepper to taste	rice mix
Melted butter	1 lb. mushrooms, sliced

Season the broilers inside and out with salt and pepper. Place on broiler pans and brush with melted butter. Bake at 350 degrees for 1 hour or until tender, brushing occasionally with butter. Cook the rice according to package directions. Saute the mushrooms in butter until tender, then stir into rice. Mound on a large platter. Arrange the broilers over the rice and garnish with parsley.

Photograph for this recipe on cover.

BAKED CHICKEN CURRY

1 3 to 3 1/2-lb. frying chicken	2 tbsp. brown sugar
1/4 c. flour	1/4 tsp. curry
1/2 tsp. garlic salt	2 tbsp. melted butter or
1/2 tsp. curry powder	margarine
1/2 tsp. monosodium glutamate	1/4 c. coconut
3 tbsp. butter or margarine	2 tbsp. chopped onion
1 1-lb. 14-oz. can fruit cocktail	

Cut the chicken into serving pieces. Mix the flour, garlic salt, curry powder and monosodium glutamate in a brown paper or plastic bag and shake the chicken in seasoned flour. Melt the butter in a large skillet. Add the chicken and cook until brown. Drain the fruit cocktail and place in a casserole. Sprinkle with brown sugar and curry. Pour the melted butter over fruit cocktail. Place the chicken in a baking dish and place in the oven. Place the curried fruit in the oven. Bake at 350 degrees for 45 minutes. Remove cover from fruit and stir in the coconut and onion gently. Pour over the chicken and serve. 4 servings.

Baked Chicken Curry (above)

CRAB NEWBURG

1/4 c. butter or margarine	1/4 tsp. nutmeg
2 1/2 tbsp. flour	2 c. light cream
3/4 tsp. salt	2 egg yolks, beaten
Dash of cayenne pepper	2 c. crab meat

Melt the butter in a saucepan, then blend in the flour and seasonings. Add the cream gradually and cook, stirring constantly, until thick and smooth. Stir a small amount of the hot sauce into the egg yolks, then stir back into the hot sauce. Add the crab meat and heat thoroughly. Serve immediately on toast points. 6 servings.

Mrs. Harold D. Mooty, Marion, Alabama

CRAB SOUFFLE

1 1/2 c. milk, scalded	1 tbsp. minced onion
1 c. soft bread crumbs	2 tbsp. minced green pepper
1/4 c. butter, melted	1 tbsp. minced pimento
1/2 c. grated cheese	4 eggs, separated
1 c. fresh crab meat	

Combine the milk, bread crumbs, butter, cheese, crab meat, onion, green pepper and pimento and mix well. Beat the egg yolks and stir into the crab mixture, then fold in the stiffly beaten egg whites. Turn into a deep baking dish. Bake at 350 degrees for 1 hour. 4-6 servings.

Mrs. Jean Carson, Fredericksburg, Virginia

TROUT AMANDINE

1 tsp. salt	Paprika to taste
1 tsp. monosodium glutamate	Juice of 1 lemon
1/8 tsp. white pepper	2 tbsp. grated lemon rind
1 c. water	1/8 c. slivered toasted
4 brook trout	almonds
3/4 c. melted butter	

Mix the salt, monosodium glutamate, pepper and water and pour into a shallow baking dish. Place the trout in the baking dish and drizzle with half the melted butter. Sprinkle with paprika. Bake in 425-degree oven for about 25 minutes or until fish flakes easily when tested with a fork. Combine remaining butter, lemon juice, lemon rind and almonds and pour over trout. Garnish with parsley sprigs, lemon wedges and cherry tomatoes.

Mrs. Elsie Bailey, Rome, Georgia

DEVILED CRAB WITH PECANS

1 c. grated sharp cheese	1 1/2 tsp. dry mustard
1 c. fine dry bread crumbs	Dash of pepper
1/2 c. chopped pecans	1/4 c. minced onion

1 sm. pimento, chopped

2 c. medium white sauce

1 tsp. Worcestershire sauce

1 drop of hot sauce

2 hard-cooked eggs, chopped

2 tbsp. chopped parsley

1 c. cooked crab

Mix 1/4 cup cheese with crumbs and pecans. Add the mustard, pepper, onion and pimento to white sauce and mix well. Add remaining cheese, Worcestershire sauce and hot sauce and cook over low heat, stirring until cheese melts. Add the eggs, parsley and crab and mix. Place half the crab mixture in a greased baking dish and cover with half the crumb mixture. Add remaining crab mixture and sprinkle remaining crumb mixture on top. Bake in 375-degree oven for about 20 minutes or until golden brown. 6 servings.

Mrs. Gordon Ritchie, Henderson, Kentucky

BARBECUED TROUT

1   3 to 4-lb. trout

Salt

2 tbsp. chopped onion

1 tbsp. shortening

1 c. catsup

2 tbsp. vinegar

1/4 c. lemon juice

3 tbsp. Worcestershire sauce

2 tbsp. brown sugar

Dash of pepper

Place the trout in a greased, shallow pan and sprinkle with salt to taste. Saute the onion in the shortening in a saucepan until tender. Add remaining ingredients and 1/2 teaspoon salt and simmer for 5 minutes. Pour over the trout. Bake at 425 degrees for 35 to 40 minutes. 6-8 servings.

Mrs. Francis Joiner, Tennille, Georgia

SOUTH GEORGIA CATFISH AND SWAMP GRAVY

3 lb. catfish steaks or

   fillets

1 1/2 tbsp. salt

1 c. cornmeal

Sprinkle the catfish with salt and coat with cornmeal. Fry in deep, hot fat until brown, then drain on absorbent paper.

Swamp Gravy

1 tbsp. cornmeal

3 c. diced potatoes

1 c. diced onion

1 No. 2 can tomatoes

1 can tomato juice

1 tsp. salt

1 tsp. pepper

Pour 1/2 cup fat into a saucepan. Add the cornmeal, potatoes and onion and cook until tender. Add remaining ingredients and cook, stirring frequently, until thickened. Serve with the catfish.

Mrs. Andy Jones, Donalsonville, Georgia

ISLAND SCALLOP CASSEROLE

2 lb. scallops	1/2 c. finely chopped celery
1 c. buttered bread crumbs	1 c. light cream
1 tsp. salt	2 tbsp. grated Parmesan
1/2 c. minced green pepper	cheese

Wash and drain the scallops. Place in a saucepan and cover with cold water. Bring to boiling point over low heat, then drain. Place 1/3 of the crumbs in a greased casserole and add half the scallops, salt, green pepper and celery. Add half the remaining crumbs, then add remaining scallops, salt, green pepper and celery. Add the cream. Mix remaining crumbs with cheese and sprinkle over casserole. Bake in 350-degree oven for 30 minutes. 6 servings.

Laura Cummings, West Point, Georgia

SHRIMP WITH CRUNCH

1 lb. peeled deveined shrimp	1/8 tsp. liquid pepper sauce
1 egg white, slightly beaten	1/4 c. finely chopped green
3/4 c. packaged corn flake	pepper
crumbs	6 tbsp. melted butter
1/4 tsp. salt	Toasted bread triangles
1/4 tsp. dry mustard	2 tbsp. lime juice
1/2 tsp. Worcestershire sauce	

Rinse the shrimp and drain on paper towels. Add to the egg white in a mixing bowl and stir until coated. Mix the crumbs, salt, mustard, Worcestershire sauce, pepper sauce, green pepper and 2 tablespoons butter. Dip the shrimp into the crumbs mixture until coated generously and arrange in a single layer in a foil-lined shallow baking dish. Bake at 350 degrees for 30 minutes. Place on bread triangles on a platter. Combine remaining butter and lime juice in a bowl and serve with the shrimp. 4 servings.

Shrimp with Crunch (above)

MARINATED SHRIMP

2 1/2 lb. shrimp	1/4 c. mixed pickling spices
1/2 c. chopped celery tops	1 onion, sliced
3 1/2 tsp. salt	4 bay leaves

Place the shrimp in a saucepan and add enough boiling water to cover. Add remaining ingredients except onion slices and bay leaves and cook for 10 minutes. Drain the shrimp, then cool and clean. Place alternate layers of shrimp and onion slices in a shallow dish, and add bay leaves.

Sauce

1 1/4 c. salad oil	2 1/2 tsp. celery salt
3/4 c. vinegar	2 1/2 tbsp. capers and juice
1 1/2 tsp. salt	Dash of hot sauce (opt.)

Combine all ingredients and pour over the shrimp mixture. Marinate in refrigerator overnight.

Mrs. Gardner Watson, Perry, Georgia

SOUTHERN-FRIED OYSTERS

1 egg	1/4 tsp. salt
1/4 c. milk	1 pt. oysters, drained
1/4 c. flour	1 c. self-rising cornmeal

Combine the egg, milk, flour and salt and mix well. Dip the oysters in egg mixture, then coat with cornmeal. Fry in deep, hot fat until golden brown.

Mrs. W. C. King, Troy, Alabama

CREAMED ONIONS WITH PECANS AND CHEESE

20 sm. onions	4 tbsp. flour
1/2 c. water	1 1/2 c. milk
1 1/2 tsp. salt	1 c. shredded cheese
4 tbsp. melted butter	1/2 c. chopped pecans

Place the onions, water and 1 teaspoon salt in a 1 1/2-quart saucepan. Cover and bring to a boil over high heat. Reduce heat and simmer for 15 minutes or until tender. Drain. Blend the butter and flour in a saucepan, then stir in the milk and remaining salt. Cook over medium heat until thickened, stirring constantly. Add the cheese and stir until melted. Add onions and heat through. Place in a serving dish and sprinkle with pecans. 4-6 servings.

Mrs. Juanita Patton, Holly Hill, South Carolina

SQUASH CASSEROLE

2 c. cooked squash	1/2 tsp. salt
1 c. milk	Pinch of pepper
1/2 c. butter or margarine	1 tbsp. sugar
2 eggs	1/2 c. grated cheese
1 c. cracker crumbs	

Combine all ingredients except cheese and place in a casserole. Top with cheese. Bake at 350 degrees for about 30 minutes or until brown.

Mrs. Ira Falls, Kings Mountain, North Carolina

BOILED OKRA

1 qt. tender okra	1 tbsp. bacon drippings or
1 tbsp. cider vinegar	butter
Salt to taste	

Cut most of the stems from okra, leaving 1/2-inch stems. Place in a saucepan and cover with cold water. Cook over low heat until heated through, then add vinegar. Simmer, without stirring, until okra is fork-tender. Drain, then add salt and bacon drippings.

Mrs. Pearl Burbank, El Dorado, Arkansas

STEWED OKRA AND TOMATOES

2 slices bacon	1 lb. peeled tomatoes,
1 lge. onion, chopped	chopped
1 med. green pepper,	1 tsp. salt
chopped	1/2 tsp. pepper
1 lb. okra, sliced	

Fry the bacon in a heavy skillet until brown, then remove from skillet. Saute the onion and green pepper in bacon drippings until tender, then add remaining ingredients. Crumble the bacon and add to the okra mixture. Cover and cook for 30 to 35 minutes. Uncover and cook for 5 minutes longer. 6 servings.

Mrs. Ina C. Hooper, Elizabeth, Louisiana

SOUTHERN BUTTERMILK BISCUITS

2 c. flour	1/4 tsp. soda
1 tsp. salt	3 tbsp. vegetable shortening
2 tsp. baking powder	3/4 c. buttermilk

Sift the dry ingredients together into a bowl and cut in shortening until mixture resembles coarse crumbs. Add the buttermilk and stir until mixed. Place on a floured surface and roll out to desired thickness. Cut with a biscuit cutter and place on a greased baking sheet. Bake at 450 degrees for 10 to 15 minutes.

Mrs. Raoul J. Kyle, Bedford, Virginia

Toasted Southern Corn Bread (below)

TOASTED SOUTHERN CORN BREAD

2 eggs, beaten	1/4 c. flour
1 tsp. soda	3 tbsp. oil
2 c. buttermilk	Butter
2 c. cornmeal	Onion salt to taste
1 tsp. salt	

Combine all the ingredients except the butter and onion salt in a mixing bowl and mix well. Pour into a hot greased square pan. Bake at 450 degrees until brown and firm. Remove from oven and cool. Cut into squares and split in half, then spread with butter. Sprinkle lightly with onion salt. Place on baking sheet and toast under broiler.

JOHNNYCAKE

1 c. flour	2 eggs, well beaten
3/4 tsp. soda	1 1/2 c. buttermilk
1 tsp. salt	3 tbsp. cooking oil
1 1/2 c. cornmeal	

Sift the flour, soda and salt together in a bowl, then add the cornmeal. Combine the eggs, buttermilk and oil and add to the cornmeal mixture, stirring until smooth. Turn into a 9 x 13-inch pan. Bake at 375 degrees for 30 minutes.

Mrs. Cary Atwood, Greeneville, Tennessee

HOE CAKES

1 c. white cornmeal	1/2 tsp. salt

Mix the cornmeal and salt in a bowl. Add enough boiling water, stirring constantly, until mixture resembles soft biscuit dough. Drop by spoonfuls into small amount of hot fat in a skillet and cook until brown. Turn and cook until brown, adding fat, if needed. Serve hot. 2-3 servings.

Doris Snedden, Globe, Arizona

COBBLESTONE COFFEE CAKE

1/2 c. milk, scalded	1/4 c. melted butter or
1/2 c. shortening	margarine
1/2 c. sugar	2/3 c. (packed) brown sugar
1/2 tsp. salt	1/2 tsp. cinnamon
1 pkg. dry yeast	1/2 c. raisins
1/4 c. warm water	1/2 c. chopped nuts
3 to 3 1/2 c. sifted flour	1/2 c. chopped mixed candied
2 eggs, beaten	fruit

Combine the milk, shortening, sugar and salt in a bowl and stir until sugar is dissolved. Cool to lukewarm. Dissolve the yeast in water, then combine with milk mixture. Stir in half the flour. Add the eggs and beat well. Add enough remaining flour to make a soft dough. Turn out on a lightly floured board and knead until smooth and elastic. Place in a greased bowl and turn to grease top. Cover and let rise in a warm place for about 2 hours or until doubled in bulk. Punch down and form into 1-inch balls. Roll each ball in butter, then in a mixture of brown sugar and cinnamon. Place a layer of balls in a greased 9-inch pan and sprinkle with raisins, nuts and fruit. Cover with another layer of balls and repeat until all dough, raisins, nuts and fruit have been used. Cover and let rise until doubled in bulk. Bake at 350 degrees for 40 minutes.

Mrs. Rogers Whittington, Van Buren, Arkansas

PEANUT-MARMALADE COFFEE CAKE

2 c. prepared biscuit mix	1 egg
1/4 c. sugar	1/2 c. orange marmalade
1/4 c. peanut butter	1/2 c. chopped salted peanuts
3/4 c. milk	

Combine the biscuit mix with sugar in a bowl and cut in peanut butter. Beat the milk and egg together and add to peanut butter mixture. Beat for about 30 seconds. Spread in a greased 10 x 6 x 2-inch pan and spread with marmalade. Sprinkle peanuts over top. Bake at 350 degrees for 25 minutes.

Icing

3/4 c. confectioners' sugar	1 tsp. vanilla
1 tbsp. milk or water	

Combine all ingredients in a bowl and mix well. Drizzle over warm cake. 6-8 servings.

Mrs. T. W. Nicholson, Eastman, Georgia

DELICIOUS PEANUT PIE

4 eggs, separated	1 c. crushed peanuts
2 tbsp. butter	3 tsp. lemon juice
2 c. sugar	1 tsp. vanilla
1 c. raisins	1 unbaked pie shell

Beat the egg yolks until light. Cream the butter and sugar together, then add the egg yolks. Stir in the raisins, peanuts, lemon juice and vanilla and mix well. Fold in lightly beaten egg whites. Turn into the pie shell. Bake at 325 degrees for 50 minutes.

Mrs. Rand Wade, Snow Hill, North Carolina

SOUTHERN PECAN PIE

1 c. flour	3/4 c. light corn syrup
Salt	3 eggs, beaten
Margarine	1 3/4 c. pecans
3 to 4 tbsp. ice water	1 tsp. vanilla
1 c. sugar	

Combine the flour and 1/2 teaspoon salt in a bowl; then cut in 1/3 cup margarine with pastry blender until mixture resembles coarse meal. Stir in the ice water and mix well. Roll out dough to fit a 9-inch pie plate on a lightly floured board. Transfer to plate and trim the edge leaving 1/2-inch overhang. Fold edge under and flute by placing left forefinger against inside of pastry rim and pinching outside with right thumb and forefinger. Repeat all around the rim. Blend the sugar, syrup and 1/2 cup margarine in a saucepan and cook over medium heat, stirring constantly, until mixture comes to a boil. Blend the hot mixture slowly into the eggs. Stir in the pecans, vanilla and 1/8 teaspoon salt. Pour into the pie shell. Bake at 375 degrees for about 30 minutes. Serve warm or cold or top with vanilla ice cream, if desired.

Southern Pecan Pie (above)

131

CARAMEL-PECAN LAYER CAKE

1/3 c. butter or shortening	3/4 tsp. salt
1 1/8 c. sugar	3/4 c. milk
2 c. sifted cake flour	1 egg
2 tsp. baking powder	1 tsp. vanilla

Place the butter in a mixing bowl and beat with electric mixer until softened. Sift the sugar, flour, baking powder and salt together and add to butter. Add the milk and mix at low speed until flour is dampened. Beat for 2 minutes at medium speed. Add egg and vanilla and beat for 1 minute longer. Pour into 2 greased and floured layer pans. Bake at 375 degrees for 25 minutes.

Quick Caramel Frosting

1/2 c. butter	1/4 c. milk
1 c. (firmly packed) brown sugar	1 3/4 c. confectioners' sugar

Melt the butter in a saucepan. Add brown sugar and cook over low heat for 2 minutes, stirring constantly. Add the milk and cook, stirring, until mixture comes to a boil. Remove from heat and cool. Add enough confectioners' sugar until of spreading consistency. Spread between layers and on top and side of cake. Garnish with pecan halves, if desired.

Mrs. Mattie Norman, Newton, Mississippi

SOUTHERN LANE CAKE

3 1/4 c. sifted flour	2 c. sugar
3 1/2 tsp. baking powder	1 tsp. vanilla
1/2 tsp. salt	1 c. milk
1 c. butter or margarine	8 egg whites, stiffly beaten

Sift the flour with baking powder and salt. Cream the butter and sugar in a bowl until light and fluffy, then add vanilla. Add the flour mixture alternately with the milk. Fold in the egg whites. Grease bottoms of four 9-inch layer pans and line with waxed paper. Pour batter into layer pans. Bake at 375 degrees for 15 to 20 minutes. Cool.

Filling

8 egg yolks, slightly beaten	1 c. chopped candied
1 1/4 c. sugar	cherries
1/2 c. butter or margarine	1/3 c. whiskey or wine
1 c. chopped pecans	1 c. chopped seedless
1 c. grated fresh coconut	raisins

Combine the egg yolks, sugar and butter in a saucepan. Cook over low heat for about 5 minutes or until slightly thickened, stirring constantly. Stir in remaining ingredients and cool. Spread between cake layers.

Frosting

2 1/2 c. sugar	2/3 c. water
1/8 tsp. salt	2 egg whites
1/3 c. dark corn syrup	1 tsp. vanilla

Combine the sugar, salt, corn syrup and water in a saucepan. Cook over low heat, stirring, until sugar dissolves. Bring to a boil without stirring. Beat the egg whites until foamy. Add 3 tablespoons syrup slowly and beat until stiff but not dry. Cook remaining syrup to hard-ball stage or 265 degrees on candy thermometer. Add to egg whites slowly, beating constantly, then beat until frosting begins to lose gloss and holds shape. Stir in vanilla and spread over top and side of cake.

Mrs. J. C. Kemp, Norfolk, Virginia

APRICOT PUREE GATEAU

2 yellow cake layers	3 c. whipped cream
2 jars junior baby food	1/2 c. chopped walnuts
apricots	Drained apricot halves

Split the cake layers in half crosswise. Place 1 layer of the cake on serving plate, then spread 1 jar of the apricots over top. Combine half the whipped cream and the walnuts and spread half the walnut mixture over the apricots. Top with another cake layer and spread with the remaining apricots. Add another cake layer, then spread with the remaining walnut mixture. Cover with the remaining cake layer. Frost the side with the remaining whipped cream. Chill for at least 3 hours, then cover top with the apricot halves. Serve immediately.

Apricot Puree Gateau (above)

SACHER CAKE

3 c. sifted flour	3 sq. unsweetened chocolate,
1 1/2 tsp. soda	melted
3/4 tsp. salt	1 1/2 c. ice water
2 1/4 c. sugar	1 jar baby food apricots
3/4 c. butter	Chocolate-Apricot Filling
1 1/2 tsp. vanilla	Chocolate Frosting
3 eggs	

Sift the flour, soda and salt together. Cream the sugar, butter and vanilla together in a large mixing bowl. Add the eggs, beating until light and fluffy. Stir in the chocolate. Add the flour mixture and water alternately, beating until smooth after each addition. Pour into 3 greased 9-inch layer pans. Bake at 350 degrees for 35 to 40 minutes or until cake tests done. Cool for 5 minutes, then remove from pans and cool on cake racks. Place layer of cake on serving plate, then spread a thin layer of apricots on top. Spread with the Filling. Add second cake layer and repeat layer of apricots and Filling. Top with the remaining cake layer. Cover top and side with the Frosting.

Chocolate-Apricot Filling

1 sq. chocolate, melted	1 jar baby food apricots
2 c. confectioners' sugar	

Combine the chocolate and confectioners' sugar in a bowl, then add enough apricots to make of spreading consistency, mixing well.

Chocolate Frosting

2 sq. chocolate, grated	1/2 c. shortening
2 c. sugar	1/2 tsp. salt
2/3 c. milk	1 tsp. vanilla

Combine all the ingredients except the vanilla in a heavy saucepan. Bring to a boil over low heat and cook for 2 minutes, stirring constantly. Remove from the heat and beat with an electric mixer until lukewarm. Add the vanilla and beat until of spreading consistency.

PEACHES AND SYLLABUB

1 c. fresh sliced peaches	1 c. whipping cream
1 tbsp. lemon juice	1 egg white
5/8 c. powdered sugar	2 tbsp. sherry

Combine the peaches, lemon juice and 2 tablespoons sugar in a bowl and set aside. Whip the cream with 1/4 cup sugar until stiff. Beat the egg white with remaining sugar until stiff and fold in whipped cream. Add sherry and place over peaches. 4 servings.

Nell W. Pantell, Jefferson, Georgia

Sacher Cake (page 134)

SPEEDY PEACH COBBLER

1/2 c. flour
1 tsp. baking powder
1/2 c. sugar
1/2 c. milk

1 tbsp. melted butter
2 c. sliced sweetened
   peaches

Mix the flour, baking powder and sugar in a bowl. Add the milk and butter and stir until mixed. Pour into a greased 1 1/2-quart casserole and spread peaches over top. Bake at 350 degrees for about 35 minutes. Serve warm with cream or ice cream. 6 servings.

Mrs. Lawrence Claiborne Brock, Liberty, Kentucky

SPECIAL PEACH PUDDING

4 c. peeled, chopped peaches
1 2/3 c. sugar
1 c. flour

1/3 c. milk
1/3 c. butter, softened
1 egg, beaten

Cover peaches with 1 cup sugar and set aside. Combine remaining sugar with remaining ingredients in a bowl and mix well. Fold in peaches and pour into well-greased deep baking dish. Bake at 350 degrees for 40 minutes and serve hot or cold with whipped cream or dessert topping. 8 servings.

Mrs. Edd L. Jones, Reidsville, North Carolina

favorite foods of alabama, mississippi, and louisiana

Alabama, Mississippi, and Louisiana represent the westernmost fringes of the Deep South, the place the regional culture and cookery is the strongest and reflects most accurately the many influences that have gone into it. Here, traditional English recipes, pioneer dishes, and the elegant French-Indian-African-Spanish Creole Louisiana mingled to produce recipes that are near-legendary.

Many of these recipes are yours to enjoy in the pages that follow. One, Squirrel Jambalaya, illustrates the blending of pioneer ingenuity with Louisianian cookery. Early settlers depended upon squirrels and other small game for sustenance. The jambalaya method of cooking, a mingling of meat and vegetables with rice is unique to Creole Louisiana. This recipe probably was developed in northern Louisiana or Mississippi when pioneer women from Georgia or Alabama had their first encounter with Louisiana-style cooking.

Other recipes you'll find in this section reflect the English influence in Deep South cookery. Scalloped Chicken and Oysters, Baked Snapper and Dressing, and Festive Fig Pudding probably have their English counterparts.

Browse now through these pages and enjoy the marvels of southern cooking. Whether your family prefers the hot bite of Creole cooking, the mildness of English-style food, or plain heartiness of pioneer dishes, you'll find recipes to please everyone.

137

A traveler through the newly-independent colonies in the days immediately following the American Revolution wrote: "A few days before we arrived at the Nation (Creek), we met a company of emigrants from Georgia; a man,

HISTORY AND TRADITIONS OF

alabama, mississippi, and louisiana

his wife, a young woman, several young children, and three stout young men, with about a dozen horses loaded with their property. They informed us their design was to settle on the Alabama, a few miles above the confluence of the Tombigbe."

These adventuresome settlers were the vanguard of a vast movement that was to sweep through western Georgia into Alabama, Mississippi, and Louisiana in the closing years of the eighteenth century and the beginning of the nineteenth. They traveled by three major routes. Some followed the Mississippi up from New Orleans or down from Ohio and established communities and plantations along the fertile river banks. Others poured down the Shenandoah, that ancient route for settlers in the Carolinas, Tennessee, and Kentucky, into northern Alabama where they found red clay soil capable of growing many crops. Still others traversed the Chattahoochee River at places like old Fort Mitchell. They crossed the river systems that even today mark Alabama and Mississippi, settling where the land was plentiful and offered an enterprising man an opportunity to make his fortune.

Most of these settlers were second and third generation Americans, moving out from the Carolinas, Georgia, and Virginia into what was the new nation's frontier. Even Louisiana, legally French territory until 1803, was filled with ambitious American settlers bent on clearing the virgin land and making it yield the crops that would bring them the fortunes that other men had made in the more settled colonies.

Among the possessions these pioneer families brought with them were the recipes and cooking pots that would one day help create Deep South cookery. But not all the settlers of this fertile region were native Americans, and the colonists who arrived from the Old World arrived with their ways of preparing food, too. Louisiana, for example, had a heavy French-Spanish population around New Orleans and a strongly French population as far north as Baton Rouge. Americans settling in these regions found that their womenfolk exchanged recipes and methods of preparation in the timeless way women have — and the cuisine began to alter accordingly.

There were small pockets of settlement in Alabama, too, like the predominantly French town of Demopolis or Greek-settled Fairhope. Both of these settlements enriched and altered the lifestyles of the settlers around them even as they themselves were adapting to the American way of life. The result was a mixture of both — and yielded some delightful recipes!

Mississippi, like Alabama and Louisiana, had its share of Old World influences from British and French settlers. Many of the British settled in the fertile black soil belt of Mississippi and sought to establish the kind of gracious English country life they had left behind them. French influences were brought by Creole women who married into Mississippi's vast landowning class or by Creole men who resettled in Mississippi when Louisiana was sold to the United States.

This frontier soon evolved a new and gracious society, one that was almost cosmopolitan in its lifestyle. Cotton was king during the years the region was settled, and cotton-based fortunes provided many plantations with the means to gracious living. Hospitality dominated plantation life: it was not unusual for year-long visits between family members or friends to be the signal for an endless round of parties and balls. The barbecue flourished as friends gathered from miles around to meet the latest visitors. French chefs prepared delicacies in kitchens carefully removed from the rest of the house lest fire should occur. Yet even here, despite barbecues and French chefs, the essentials of Deep South cuisine dominated every other element.

BAKED DUCK WITH OYSTER DRESSING

1 lge. duck	Leaves from 1 bunch celery,
Salt to taste	chopped
1 loaf bread	1 pt. oysters, drained
4 eggs, beaten	

Place the duck and giblets in a kettle and add 2 quarts boiling water and salt. Simmer for 1 hour, adding water, if needed. Drain the duck and giblets and reserve broth. Break the bread in small pieces. Add the eggs, celery leaves and oysters. Chop the giblets and add to bread mixture. Add enough hot broth to moisten and mix well. Place in a casserole. Place the duck in a roaster and add small amount of water. Cover. Bake the duck and dressing at 350 degrees for 1 hour or until duck is tender. 6 servings.

Mrs. Ted Wilson, McAlester, Oklahoma

BRAISED CHICKEN

1 broiler, halved	1/2 stick margarine
Salt and pepper to taste	Juice of 1 lemon
Celery salt to taste	1/2 tsp. Worcestershire
Onion salt to taste	sauce
Garlic salt to taste	1/4 c. water

Season the broiler with salt and pepper, then sprinkle generously with celery salt. Sprinkle lightly with onion salt and garlic salt. Melt the margarine in a heavy skillet, then add the broiler and brown on both sides. Add the remaining ingredients and cover tightly. Simmer for 45 to 60 minutes or until tender. 2 servings.

Mrs. Charles M. Pitchford, Greenwood, Mississippi

SCALLOPED CHICKEN AND OYSTERS

1 sm. chicken, cooked	2 lb. fresh mushrooms, sliced
Saltine cracker crumbs	4 1/2 doz. large oysters
Butter	Chicken broth
Salt and pepper to taste	Milk

Remove the chicken from the bones and cut in bite-sized pieces. Arrange a layer of crumbs in a large casserole. Dot generously with butter, then sprinkle with salt and pepper. Add the chicken and cover with sliced mushrooms. Sprinkle with salt and pepper. Add a layer of crumbs and dot with butter. Add the oysters and sprinkle with salt and pepper. Top with layer of crumbs and butter. Mix equal parts of chicken broth and milk and pour in enough to almost cover casserole. Bake, uncovered, at 350 degrees for 45 minutes. Broil for 5 minutes or until browned. 8 servings.

Mrs. John P. Norman, West Point, Georgia

SOUTHERN-FRIED CHICKEN

1 fryer, disjointed	1/2 c. evaporated milk
Salt to taste	Flour
1 egg, well beaten	

Season the fryer with salt. Mix the egg with the milk and pour over the fryer. Let stand for 10 minutes. Roll in flour and fry in hot fat over medium heat until golden brown.

Mrs. Lillian McDaniel, Tinesman, Arkansas

CORNISH HENS WITH ORANGE-RICE STUFFING

1 lge. can mandarin oranges	1 c. melted butter
1 c. rice	4 Cornish hens
1 tsp. curry powder	1/2 c. white wine
1 tbsp. chopped parsley	

Drain the oranges and reserve the juice. Cook the rice according to package directions, using the reserved juice as part of the water. Stir in the curry powder, parsley, 1/2 cup butter and the oranges. Stuff the hens lightly, then secure opening with skewers. Place on a broiler pan. Combine the remaining butter and the wine, then brush the hens generously with the butter mixture. Bake at 350 degrees for 1 hour to 1 hour and 15 minutes, basting frequently with the butter mixture.

Clockwise from left: Goose Stuffed with Sauerkraut (page 142), Roasters with Parsley Rice (page 142), Cornish Hens with Orange-Rice Stuffing (above)

ROASTERS WITH PARSLEY RICE

1 box wild and long grain rice	2 roaster chickens
1/4 c. fresh chopped parsley	Salt and pepper to taste

Cook the rice according to package directions, then stir in the parsley. Stuff the chickens lightly with the rice and place in a greased baking pan with a small amount of water. Sprinkle with salt and pepper. Bake, covered, at 350 degrees for 1 hour. Uncover and bake 30 minutes longer or until tender.

Photograph for this recipe on page 141.

GOOSE STUFFED WITH SAUERKRAUT

1 goose	3 apples, grated
1/2 lb. bacon, diced	Salt and pepper to taste
2 lge. cans sauerkraut	

Place the goose in a baking pan. Bake at 400 degrees for 20 minutes. Fry the bacon until crisp in a skillet, then remove the bacon and drain. Pour off all the drippings except 1/4 cup, then add the sauerkraut and apples to skillet. Cook for 10 minutes. Add the bacon and toss. Season the goose with salt and pepper, then stuff cavity with half the sauerkraut mixture. Cover. Bake at 300 degrees until goose is tender and legs move easily. Place the goose on a platter. Reheat the remaining sauerkraut mixture and arrange around the goose.

Photograph for this recipe on page 141.

POT-ROASTED DOVE

6 dove	1/4 c. salad oil
Salt and pepper to taste	1 tbsp. flour
1 clove of garlic, minced	1/4 c. sherry
1/2 sm. onion, chopped	1 tbsp. chopped onion tops
1 tsp. minced green pepper	1 tbsp. minced parsley
1 stalk celery, chopped	1 can mushrooms
1 tbsp. chopped ham skin	

Season the dove with salt and pepper. Combine the garlic, onion, green pepper, celery and ham skin and stuff in the dove, then brown the dove in the hot oil in a skillet. Remove the dove from the skillet and stir in the flour and salt and pepper to taste. Brown the flour mixture lightly. Return the dove to the skillet and add 2 cups water and the sherry. Cover and simmer until the dove is tender. Add the onion tops, parsley and mushrooms, then cook for 10 minutes longer. Serve with rice.

Mrs. Bennett Harrington, Crowley, Louisiana

Cherry-Glazed Ham (below)

CHERRY-GLAZED HAM

1 7-lb. fully cooked ham	1/2 c. orange juice
1 8-oz. jar red maraschino cherries	1/2 tsp. whole cloves
1 c. (firmly packed) brown sugar	2 med. oranges, sliced and halved

Place the ham in a baking pan. Bake at 325 degrees for 1 hour and 30 minutes. Drain the cherries, reserving the syrup. Combine the brown sugar, reserved cherry syrup, orange juice and whole cloves in a saucepan, and cook, stirring occasionally, until slightly thickened. Remove the ham from oven, then score and decorate with cherries and orange slices, secured with toothpicks. Brush with the glaze and bake for 30 minutes longer, brushing frequently with the glaze. Place ham on platter and garnish with parsley.

Cherry Parsley Relish

1 4-oz. jar red maraschino cherries	1 8 1/2-oz. can pineapple tidbits, drained
1 c. diced celery	2/3 c. chopped parsley

Drain and cut the cherries in half. Combine all the ingredients in a bowl and mix well. Chill for several hours, then serve with the ham.

Beef Croquettes (below), Beef Stew with Dumplings (page 145)

BEEF CROQUETTES

2 c. ground cooked beef	1/8 tsp. pepper
1/4 c. minced onion	1 c. milk
2 tbsp. chopped parsley	Fine dry bread crumbs
1/4 c. margarine	1 egg
1/4 c. flour	Peanut oil
3/4 tsp. salt	

Combine the beef, onion and parsley in a bowl. Melt the margarine in small heavy saucepan, then blend in the flour, salt and pepper. Cook over low heat, stirring, until mixture is smooth and bubbly. Remove from heat; stir in milk gradually. Return to the heat and bring to a boil, stirring constantly. Cook for 1 minute longer. Blend into beef mixture. Refrigerate for several hours or overnight. Divide the mixture into 8 portions and shape into cones, then roll in bread crumbs. Beat the egg with 2 tablespoons water, then dip the croquettes into the egg mixture. Roll again in bread crumbs. Fry in hot deep oil for about 2 to 3 minutes or until golden brown. Drain on paper towels.

Tomato Sauce

2 tbsp. margarine	1 tbsp. flour
1 tbsp. minced onion	1 c. tomato sauce

1/2 tsp. sugar
1/4 tsp. salt
1/8 tsp. crushed thyme

Dash of pepper
Dash of Worcestershire sauce

Melt the margarine in a small saucepan, then add the onion and saute until transparent. Stir in the flour until blended. Remove from heat and stir in the tomato sauce. Add the sugar and seasonings, then simmer, stirring constantly, until thickened. Serve over the croquettes.

BEEF STEW WITH DUMPLINGS

1 1/2 lb. lean beef chuck
1/4 c. flour
Margarine
1 c. sliced onion
2 lge. cloves of garlic,
    minced
1/4 c. chopped parsley
1 tbsp. salt
1/8 tsp. pepper

1 bay leaf
2 c. cubed potatoes
1 1/2 c. 1-in. carrot strips
1 c. sliced celery
1/2 c. chopped green pepper
1 c. sliced fresh mushrooms
1 1/2 c. biscuit mix
1/2 c. milk

Trim and cut the beef into 1-inch cubes, then coat with flour. Melt 1/4 cup margarine in a Dutch oven or large heavy saucepan, then add the beef and brown well. Remove the beef and set aside. Cook the onion and garlic in margarine until onion is tender, then return the beef and add 2 cups water, parsley, salt, pepper and bay leaf. Cover and simmer for 1 hour, stirring occasionally and adding water if needed. Add the potatoes, carrots, celery and green pepper and cover. Simmer for 15 minutes longer, then add the mushrooms. Combine the biscuit mix, milk and 3 tablespoons melted margarine and stir until just blended. Drop by tablespoonfuls onto the stew. Simmer, uncovered, for 10 minutes. Cover and simmer for 10 minutes longer. 4-5 servings.

Photograph for this recipe on page 144.

HERBED PORK HEARTS

Pork hearts
Flour
Chopped onion to taste
1 c. water or stock

Herb seasoning to taste
1 pimento, chopped
Salt and pepper to taste
1 recipe biscuit dough

Cut the hearts in thin slices across grain and dredge with flour. Saute the hearts and onion in small amount of fat until brown. Place in a casserole and add the water, herb seasoning, pimento, salt and pepper. Cover. Bake at 350 degrees for 1 hour and 30 minutes or until done. Remove cover. Drop the biscuit dough by spoonfuls on top and bake until biscuits are brown.

Terry Jean Tims, Durant, Mississippi

145

PORK CHOP DUMPLINGS

4 pork chops	**1 can buttermilk biscuits**
Salt to taste	**Dash of pepper**

Season the chops with salt, then place in a skillet and cover with water. Cook until tender. Spoon off excess fat. Roll the biscuits out thin on a floured board, then cut into strips. Bring the liquid and chops to a boil, adding water if needed, then drop in the strips. Cover and cook until done. Sprinkle with pepper before serving. 4 servings.

Cordie Waycaster, Greenwood Springs, Mississippi

SAUSAGE PATTIES WITH SWEET POTATOES

2 c. mashed sweet potatoes	**8 sausage patties**
1/2 c. (packed) brown sugar	

Fill a deep buttered pie plate with sweet potatoes, then sprinkle lightly with brown sugar. Brown the sausage in a skillet, then place over the sugar. Add a small amount of the drippings to the top. Bake in 350-degree oven for 15 to 20 minutes. 4 servings.

Mrs. H. T. Pippin, Hartford, Alabama

SOUTHERN-STYLE SMOTHERED STRIPS

1 lge. onion, cut in wedges	**1 2-oz. can pimentos**
2 green peppers, cut in strips	**2 tbsp. lemon juice**
1/2 c. vegetable oil	**1 tsp. salt**
2 lb. beef tenderloin, cut in strips	**1/2 tsp. pepper**

Cook the onion and green peppers in oil in a skillet until tender. Add the beef and cook until brown. Drain pimentos, chop and add to the beef mixture. Season with lemon juice, salt and pepper and cook for several minutes longer.

Mrs. John Roberts, Lineville, Alabama

STEAK WITH BUTTER-CRUMB DUMPLINGS

2 lb. round steak	**1 soup can water**
1/3 c. flour	**1/2 tsp. salt**
1/4 c. shortening	**1/8 tsp. pepper**
1 can cream of chicken soup	

Cut the steak in 6 portions and dredge with flour. Brown steak lightly in shortening in a large skillet, then place in a 2-quart baking dish. Mix the soup, water, salt and pepper in the same skillet and bring to a boil. Pour over the steak. Bake at 350 degrees for 30 minutes or until steak is tender. Remove from oven and increase temperature to 425 degrees.

Butter-Crumb Dumplings

1 c. fine dry bread crumbs	1 tsp. poultry seasoning
1/2 c. melted butter	1/2 tsp. salt
2 c. flour	1 c. milk
3 tsp. baking powder	

Mix the bread crumbs and 1/4 cup butter. Combine the flour, baking powder, poultry seasoning and salt in a bowl. Pour in milk and remaining butter and stir until dry ingredients are moistened. Drop by rounded spoonfuls into buttered crumbs and roll until coated. Place on top of steak mixture and bake for 20 to 30 minutes longer. 6 servings.

Mrs. H. H. Tippins, Griffin, Georgia

SQUIRREL JAMBALAYA

4 squirrels, disjointed	2 cloves of garlic, minced
2 c. chopped onions	2 c. rice
1/2 c. chopped celery	3 tbsp. chopped green onions
1/2 c. chopped green pepper	Salt and pepper to taste

Brown the squirrels in a Dutch oven in about 1/2 cup hot fat. Add the onions, celery, green pepper and garlic and cook until the vegetables are tender. Add 3 1/2 cups water, rice, green onions, salt and pepper, then cover. Simmer for about 1 hour or until the squirrel is tender. 8 servings.

Miss Euther Hughes, Baton Rouge, Louisiana

GRANDMERE'S VEAL PIE

1 1/2 lb. veal, cut in cubes	1 tsp. salt
3 tbsp. shortening	1/8 tsp. pepper
3 tbsp. flour	2 hard-cooked eggs, chopped
1 med. onion, chopped	1/2 tsp. sage
1 carrot, sliced	1 recipe pie pastry
1 med. potato, diced	Milk
2 c. water	

Brown the veal in shortening in a skillet and stir in the flour. Add the onion, carrot, potato, water and seasonings and cook over medium heat until thick. Place half the veal mixture in a 10 x 6 1/2-inch baking dish and cover with eggs. Sprinkle with sage and add remaining veal mixture. Cover with pastry and brush with milk. Bake at 350 degrees for 1 hour to 1 hour and 20 minutes. 6-8 servings.

Mrs. Delphine S. Hooker, Durham, North Carolina

SEAFOOD GUMBO

1 6-in. slice salt pork	1 tsp. salt
1/2 pkg. sliced okra	1 bay leaf
1 onion, chopped	1/2 tsp. garlic salt
2 tbsp. flour	Dash of pepper
1 pt. canned tomatoes	Dash of cayenne pepper
1 doz. oysters and liquor	1 can crab meat
1 1/2 qt. boiling water	1 lb. shelled shrimp
2 sprigs of parsley	1 tbsp. file

Fry the salt pork in a skillet until crisp, then remove from the skillet and chop. Saute the okra in pan drippings, then add the onion and fry until tender, stirring constantly. Push the vegetables to one side of skillet, then brown the flour. Mix the onion and okra into the flour and add the tomatoes, oyster liquor and boiling water gradually, stirring constantly, until smooth. Add the seasonings and stir well, then simmer for 1 hour. Add the salt pork, crab meat and shrimp and simmer for several minutes longer. Add the oysters and simmer for 15 minutes. Stir in the file just before serving. Serve in soup bowls over rice. 6 servings.

Annie G. Childress, Mangham, Louisiana

TURTLE SOUP A LA NEW ORLEANS

3 lb. chopped turtle meat	2 sprigs of parsley
1 c. finely chopped onion	1 sprig of thyme
2 cloves of garlic,	Salt and pepper to taste
chopped (opt.)	1 tbsp. whole allspice
3 tbsp. cooking oil	1 tbsp. whole cloves
2 tbsp. flour	3 hard-cooked eggs, sliced
1 6-oz. can tomato paste	1 lemon, sliced
2 bay leaves	

Wash the turtle meat thoroughly and set aside. Saute the onion and garlic in oil, then add the flour and brown lightly. Add the tomato paste and simmer for 3 minutes. Add 2 quarts boiling water, bay leaves, parsley, thyme, salt, pepper and turtle meat. Tie the allspice and cloves in a cloth bag and drop into the mixture. Simmer for 1 hour or until turtle is tender. Remove the spice bag. Add the eggs and lemon and simmer for 5 minutes longer. Let stand for 1 hour. Sherry to taste may be added when served, if desired. 6 servings.

Mrs. Louis Dutel, New Orleans, Louisiana

JELLIED FRUIT AND PEANUT SALAD

1 1/2 tbsp. unflavored gelatin	2 c. orange juice
1/4 c. cold water	3 tbsp. lemon juice
1/2 c. boiling water	1/2 c. roasted peanuts
1/2 c. sugar	Lettuce leaves
1 c. diced apple	1 c. whipped cream

Soak the gelatin in cold water for 5 minutes. Add the boiling water and sugar and stir until dissolved. Add the apple, orange juice, lemon juice and peanuts and mix well. Place in 6 individual molds rinsed with cold water and chill until firm. Remove from molds and arrange on lettuce. Garnish with whipped cream.

Mrs. Alice Benton, Robert Lee, Texas

CHICKEN-RAISIN SALAD

1 lge. red apple, diced	1 1/2 c. sliced celery
3/4 c. seedless raisins	1/3 c. mayonnaise
1 1/2 c. cooked diced chicken	1 1/2 tbsp. lemon juice

Combine the apple, raisins, chicken and celery and mix well. Blend the mayonnaise and lemon juice together and stir lightly into the salad mixture. 5 servings.

Mrs. Georgie Thorne, Slocomb, Alabama

PRIME PORK SALAD

2 env. unflavored gelatin	Dash of monosodium glutamate
2 1/2 c. milk	1/2 tsp. grated onion
1/4 c. butter	3 c. diced cooked pork
3 tbsp. flour	1 c. thinly sliced celery
1 1/2 c. salad dressing	1/2 c. sliced stuffed olives
1/2 tsp. salt	1/2 c. slivered blanched almonds
1/2 c. diced unpeeled apple	3/4 c. heavy cream, whipped
Dash of pepper	

Soften the gelatin in 1/2 cup milk. Melt the butter in a saucepan over low heat and blend in flour. Add remaining milk and cook until smooth, stirring constantly. Add gelatin mixture and mix well. Blend in the salad dressing and chill until thickened. Fold in remaining ingredients and pour into a ring mold. Refrigerate until firm. 6-8 servings.

Mrs. W. G. Grove, New Orleans, Louisiana

TWELVE-HOUR MARINATED GREEN BEANS

2 lge. white onions	4 tbsp. salad oil
1 c. sugar	2 cloves of garlic
3/4 c. white vinegar	2 No. 2 cans whole green beans

Slice the onions and separate into rings. Place the sugar, vinegar, oil and garlic in a saucepan and heat, stirring, until sugar is dissolved. Cool. Drain the beans. Place alternate layers of beans and onion rings in a bowl and pour vinegar mixture over bean mixture. Cover and chill for 12 hours. Will keep in refrigerator for 2 weeks. 6 servings.

Mrs. Jessie W. Adams, Pensacola, Florida

Three-Leaf Apple Salad Plate (below)

THREE-LEAF APPLE SALAD PLATE

1 14-oz. can artichoke hearts	6 Washington State apples
1 4-oz. can pimentos	3 celery hearts, cooked
1 2-oz. jar green olives	1 c. cooked peas
1 1/2 to 2 c. tart French dressing	1 c. cooked shrimp
	18 lettuce cups

Drain the artichoke hearts, pimentos and olives. Chop the pimentos and slice the olives. Pour about 1/2 cup French dressing in each of 3 shallow bowls. Core and dice 2 apples and add to French dressing in 1 bowl along with the artichoke hearts and pimento. Core and dice 2 apples and add to French dressing in the second bowl. Cut the celery hearts in half lengthwise, then in half crosswise and combine with apples. Add the olives. Core and dice remaining apples and combine with peas and shrimp in third bowl of dressing. Marinate all mixtures in refrigerator for 3 to 4 hours. Arrange 3 lettuce cups on each salad plate. Drain the artichoke mixture and mound in 1 cup on each plate. Drain the celery mixture and arrange in the second cup. Drain the shrimp mixture and mound in the third cup. Reserve the French dressing from all mixtures. Serve the salad plates with the reserved French dressing. One-third cup of the French dressing may be blended with sour cream and served as a dressing.

COQUILLES ST. JACQUES

1/2 lb. mushrooms, sliced	1/8 tsp. dried thyme
3 tbsp. butter or margarine	1 bay leaf
1 1/2 tbsp. lemon juice	1/4 tsp. salt
1/2 c. white wine	Dash of pepper

1/2 lb. scallops, sliced

1 tbsp. flour

1/2 c. heavy cream

1 c. buttered bread crumbs

Saute the mushrooms in 2 tablespoons butter and the lemon juice until tender. Combine the wine, seasonings and scallops in a saucepan and simmer for 5 minutes. Melt the remaining butter in a saucepan and stir in the flour, then cook, stirring, for 2 minutes. Remove from heat and add the cream. Bring the sauce quickly to a boil, then remove from heat. Combine the mushrooms, scallops and sauce, then turn into individual casseroles. Sprinkle with the crumbs. Bake at 400 degrees for about 10 minutes or until browned.

Mrs. Ann McKinney, Talladega, Alabama

SHRIMP MOUSSE

2 tbsp. gelatin

1 can tomato soup

3   3-oz. packages cream
    cheese, softened

1 c. finely chopped celery

1/2 c. grated onion

2 tsp. hot sauce

4 tsp. dry mustard

1 lb. cooked shrimp

1 c. mayonnaise

Soften the gelatin in 1/2 cup cold water for about 5 minutes. Heat tomato soup in a saucepan to boiling point but do not boil. Add the gelatin to hot soup and stir until dissolved. Add the cheese, then beat with rotary beater until smooth. Add the celery, onion, hot sauce, mustard and shrimp. Chill until thickened, then fold in the mayonnaise. Pour into a greased mold and chill until firm. Unmold onto a bed of lettuce and fill center with curled celery, carrots, radishes and spring onions, if desired.

Mrs. Rita Nail, Baxley, Georgia

CREOLE-STUFFED CRABS

1 egg, beaten

1 c. milk

6 slices toast, cubed

2 tbsp. minced onion

2 tbsp. minced celery

2 tbsp. minced bell pepper

1 clove of garlic, minced

2 tbsp. butter

1 lb. fresh crab meat

2 tbsp. finely chopped
    parsley

Salt and pepper to taste

Bread crumbs

Thin lemon slices

Combine the egg and milk in a bowl, then add the toast and let stand. Saute the onion, celery, bell pepper and garlic in the butter. Add the crab meat, parsley, salt, pepper and the toast mixture and mix thoroughly. Place in 6 large crab shells and sprinkle with bread crumbs, then dot with additional butter. Place lemon slices on top. Garnish with paprika. Bake at 350 degrees for 15 minutes or until browned.

Mrs. Sam Lamartina, Lake Charles, Louisiana

Hot Crab-Avocado Casseroles (below)

HOT CRAB-AVOCADO CASSEROLES

2 California avocados	1/4 tsp. crushed red pepper
Lemon juice	1/4 tsp. crumbled thyme
2 7 1/2-oz. cans crab meat	2 c. milk
1/4 c. butter or margarine	2 tbsp. white wine
3 tbsp. flour	1/2 c. grated Parmesan cheese
1 tsp. salt	

Cut the avocados into halves lengthwise and remove seeds and skin. Cut 4 or 5 lengthwise slices for garnish and dice remaining avocados. Coat the diced and sliced avocado with lemon juice. Drain and flake the crab meat. Melt the butter in a saucepan and blend in flour, salt, pepper and thyme. Stir in the milk and cook over low heat, stirring, until mixture comes to a boil. Stir in the crab meat and wine and heat through. Stir in the diced avocado. Turn into 4 or 5 individual casseroles and sprinkle with cheese. Broil for 2 minutes or until golden brown. Garnish with the sliced avocado and serve at once. 4-5 servings.

SHRIMP ETOUFFE

1 med. onion, finely chopped	1/4 c. minced celery
	1/2 c. butter
2 green onions, finely chopped	2 tbsp. flour
	1 1/4 c. tomato sauce
3 cloves of garlic, minced	2 bay leaves

1 tbsp. Worcestershire sauce
4 drops of hot sauce
1 tsp. salt
1/2 tsp. sugar
1/2 tsp. thyme

1/8 tsp. pepper
1 lb. cleaned shrimp
2 hard-cooked eggs,
    quartered

Saute the onion, green onions, garlic and celery in butter in a large skillet until tender. Stir in the flour and cook, stirring, until lightly browned. Add 2 1/2 cups water, tomato sauce, bay leaves, Worcestershire sauce, hot sauce and seasonings. Simmer, stirring occasionally, for 25 minutes. Add the shrimp and continue cooking for 15 minutes. Turn into a serving dish and garnish with quartered eggs. Serve with hot rice. 6 servings.

Ann Townsend, Columbus, Mississippi

CRAWFISH A LA NEWBURG

2 lb. crawfish
12 whole allspice
1 bay leaf
1/4 tsp. pepper
1 tsp. salt
3 tbsp. butter
2 tbsp. flour

1 c. light cream
1/2 c. milk
3 tbsp. catsup
2 tsp. Worcestershire sauce
1/4 tsp. garlic salt
1/4 tsp. paprika
3 tbsp. sherry

Place the crawfish in a kettle and half cover with boiling water. Add the allspice, bay leaf, pepper and salt. Cover and cook for 20 minutes. Drain and cool. Shell the crawfish and cut into small pieces. Melt the butter in a double boiler and stir in the flour until smooth, then add the cream gradually, stirring constantly. Add the milk and cook, stirring constantly, until thickened and smooth. Add the catsup and Worcestershire sauce. Combine all the ingredients except the sherry and heat thoroughly. Add the sherry just before serving. 4 servings.

Mrs. Marguerite Brock, Ft. Pierce, Florida

BAYOU JAMBALAYA

2 lb. fresh shrimp
Salt and pepper to taste
3 tbsp. butter
1 tbsp. flour
1 green pepper, finely
    chopped
6 scallions, finely chopped

4 stalks celery, finely
    chopped
2 doz. oysters
1 1/2 c. diced cooked ham
1 c. diced cooked chicken
4 c. cooked rice

Shell and clean shrimp, then place in a saucepan and cover with cold water. Season with salt and pepper. Cook for 5 minutes, or until shrimp turn pink, then drain, reserving 3/4 cup stock. Melt the butter in a skillet, then stir in the flour. Blend in the reserved stock, vegetables and oysters. Simmer until the oysters curl, then add the shrimp, ham, chicken and rice. Stir until heated through. Garnish with parsley, hearts of celery, radishes and scallions, if desired. 8-10 servings.

Mrs. J. E. Sadler, Hueytown, Alabama

SHRIMP McLEAN

3 lb. fresh shrimp in shells	Freshly ground pepper to
1 5-oz. bottle	taste
Worcestershire sauce	Lemon juice to taste
1 lb. margarine	

Wash the shrimp and remove the heads and abdominal feet. Place in a casserole. Add the remaining ingredients. Bake at 350 degrees for 45 minutes. Serve in individual bowls, spooning the butter sauce over the shrimp. Serve with French bread for dunking, tossed green salad and cold beer.

Mrs. H. H. Tippins, Griffin, Georgia

OYSTERS BIENVILLE

1 bunch green onions and	1 tsp. salt
tops, minced	1 tbsp. horseradish
2 tbsp. butter or margarine	Dash of cayenne pepper
2 tbsp. flour	Ice cream salt
2/3 c. chicken broth	2 doz. oysters on
1/3 c. minced cooked	half shell, drained
mushrooms	1/2 c. French bread crumbs
1 egg yolk, beaten	1 tbsp. Parmesan cheese

Saute the onions and tops in butter over low heat for 6 minutes or until tender. Add the flour and cook, stirring, for 3 minutes or until brown. Add the broth and mushrooms and cook, stirring constantly, until thickened. Stir a small amount of the hot mixture into the egg, then stir back into hot mixture. Add the salt, horseradish and cayenne pepper. Cook for 10 to 15 minutes over low heat, stirring constantly. Place a pan of ice cream salt in oven for 30 minutes at 400 degrees. Nestle the oysters on half shell in the hot salt. Bake for 5 minutes. Spoon the sauce over each oyster. Combine the crumbs and cheese, then sprinkle over the oysters. Bake for 15 minutes or until crumbs are light brown. 4 servings.

Mrs. Jessie Mae Speights, Crosby, Mississippi

OYSTERS SUPREME

1 stick butter	2 tbsp. flour
1/2 med. green pepper,	1 sm. can mushrooms
minced	1 pt. oysters
1 bunch scallions, minced	

Preheat an electric skillet to 325 degrees. Add the butter and melt, then add the green pepper and scallions. Saute until tender, then stir in the flour. Add the mushrooms and oysters, then cook, stirring frequently, for about 10 minutes or until oysters curl. Serve on toasted French bread. 4 servings.

Agnes V. Wiedemeyer, Sheffield, Alabama

LOUISIANA FROGS' LEGS

1 c. flour   12 lge. frogs' legs
Salt and pepper to taste

Combine the flour, salt and pepper in a bag, then add the frogs' legs and shake to coat well. Remove and shake off excess flour. Fry in hot deep fat until golden brown. Drain and serve.

Mrs. Mary Casper, Baton Rouge, Louisiana

HERBED SHRIMP DIABLE

1 tsp. parsley flakes   2 lb. fresh shrimp
2 tsp. freeze-dried chives   1/2 c. butter
1/2 tsp. tarragon leaves   1/2 lb. fresh mushrooms,
1/2 tsp. ginger   sliced
1 tsp. dry mustard   12 cherry tomatoes, stems
2 tsp. season-all   removed
1/8 tsp. garlic powder   1 c. sliced celery
1/4 tsp. monosodium glutamate   3 tbsp. lemon juice
1/4 tsp. pepper   1/4 c. brandy, heated

Mix the seasonings. Shell and devein the shrimp. Melt the butter in a large skillet. Add the mushrooms, tomatoes and celery and saute for 2 to 3 minutes. Push to one side of the skillet. Add the shrimp and sprinkle with mixed seasonings. Cook for 2 minutes, stirring constantly. Add the lemon juice and mix well. Cover and simmer for 5 minutes. Place in a chafing dish. Add the brandy and ignite. Serve over rice. 4-6 servings.

Herbed Shrimp Diable (above)

SHRIMP CREOLE

2 tbsp. bacon drippings	3 bay leaves
2 tbsp. margarine	1 tbsp. chili powder
1 onion, chopped	Salt and pepper to taste
1 stalk celery, chopped	Dash of paprika
1/4 green pepper,	Dash of hot sauce
chopped	2 lb. shelled fresh shrimp
1 No. 2 can tomatoes	2 tbsp. flour
3 cloves of garlic, pressed	

Combine the bacon drippings and margarine in a deep skillet, then add the onion, celery and green pepper. Saute lightly, then add the tomatoes, garlic, bay leaves, chili powder, salt, pepper, paprika and hot sauce. Simmer for 30 to 40 minutes, stirring occasionally. Add the shrimp and cook for 15 minutes longer. Blend the flour with a small amount of water, then stir into the shrimp mixture. Simmer, stirring, until thickened. Serve over rice. 4 servings.

Mrs. Raymond L. Little, Montgomery, Alabama

BROCCOLI WITH MUSTARD SAUCE

1 pkg. frozen broccoli	1 tbsp. prepared musta.,
2 tbsp. butter	1 egg yolk, beaten
1 tsp. salt	3/4 c. milk
1/8 tsp. pepper	2 tsp. lemon juice
1 tbsp. flour	

Cook the broccoli according to package directions and drain. Melt the butter in a saucepan and stir in salt, pepper and flour. Combine the mustard, egg yolk and milk, then stir into the flour mixture. Cook for 5 minutes, stirring constantly, until thickened. Stir in the lemon juice. Pour over the hot broccoli.

Sandra Brown, Troy, Alabama

DELTA RICE

1 c. long grain rice	2 stalks celery and leaves,
4 tbsp. melted butter	chopped
2 1/2 c. boiling chicken	3 sprigs of parsley, chopped
broth	1 sm. can button mushrooms
1 med. onion, chopped	1/2 c. slivered almonds
1 green pepper, chopped	1/4 tsp. powdered oregano
1 clove of garlic, chopped	

Saute the rice in 2 tablespoons butter until golden. Pour into a 2-quart casserole, then add the broth and cover. Bake at 350 degrees for 30 minutes. Cook the onion, green pepper, garlic, celery and parsley in the remaining butter until soft and clear, then stir into the rice. Add the remaining ingredients and bake for 30 minutes longer. 6 servings.

Mrs. William A. Rucker, Pine Bluff, Arkansas

Pecan Logs with Cucumber Sauce (below)

PECAN LOGS WITH CUCUMBER SAUCE

1 env. instant mashed potatoes	1 tbsp. lemon juice
2 tbsp. chopped onion	1 tsp. salt
2 tbsp. butter or margarine	1 tsp. Worcestershire sauce
2 c. chopped pecans	Dash of pepper
2 eggs	1 tbsp. water
2 tbsp. chopped parsley	1/2 c. fine dry bread crumbs

Prepare the potatoes according to package directions, reducing water by 1/4 cup. Fry the onion in butter in a saucepan until tender. Add the potatoes, pecans, 1 egg, parsley, lemon juice, salt, Worcestershire sauce and pepper and mix well. Shape into 8 logs 3 inches long and 1 inch thick. Beat remaining egg with water. Roll the logs in crumbs. Dip in the egg mixture, then roll in crumbs. Fry in shallow, hot fat for 5 to 8 minutes or until brown on all sides.

Cucumber Sauce

2 tbsp. butter or margarine	Dash of pepper
2 tbsp. chopped green onion	1 1/4 c. milk
1 tbsp. flour	1 c. chopped pared cucumber
1/2 tsp. salt	1 tbsp. chopped parsley
1/2 tsp. dried dillweed	

Melt the butter in a saucepan. Add the onion and cook over low heat until soft. Blend in the flour, salt, dillweed and pepper. Add the milk and cook, stirring constantly, until thickened and smooth. Add the cucumber and parsley and heat through. Serve with Pecan Logs.

CHANTILLY POTATOES

5 med. potatoes, cubed	4 tbsp. butter
1/2 tsp. rosemary	1/2 c. shredded cheese
Salt and pepper to taste	1/2 c. milk

Place half the potatoes in a greased casserole, then add the seasonings, butter and half the cheese. Add the remaining potatoes and cover with milk. Add the remaining cheese. Bake at 350 degrees for 1 hour. 6-8 servings.

Mrs. Nancy Oswald, Montgomery, Alabama

DEVILED ENGLISH PEAS

1 1-lb. can English peas, drained	1 c. grated cheese
4 hard-cooked eggs, sliced	1 can cream of mushroom soup
1/2 c. chopped pimento	1/2 No. 2 can French-fried onion rings

Arrange half the peas, egg slices, pimento and cheese in layers in a casserole. Spread half the soup over top, then repeat the layers. Bake at 350 degrees for 15 minutes. Cover with onion rings and bake until heated through and browned.

Mrs. John T. Rummell, West Point, Mississippi

CRACKLING CORN BREAD

1 1/2 c. cornmeal	2 c. buttermilk
1/4 c. flour	1 egg, beaten
1 tsp. soda	1 c. finely cut cracklings
1 tsp. salt	

Sift the dry ingredients together in a bowl, then add the buttermilk and egg and stir until well blended. Fold in the cracklings. Pour into a hot greased skillet or muffin tins. Bake at 450 degrees for 25 minutes or until brown. 6 servings.

Mildred Edwards, Hamburg, Arkansas

EASY FRENCH BREAD

1 pkg. yeast	1 tbsp. shortening
1 tbsp. sugar	4 c. sifted all-purpose flour
1 1/2 tsp. salt	

Dissolve the yeast in 1/2 cup warm water. Combine the sugar, salt and shortening in a large bowl, then add 1 cup hot water, stirring until sugar is dissolved. Cool to lukewarm, then blend in the yeast. Add the flour, stirring until dough forms ball. Let dough rise, stirring down 5 times at 10-minute intervals. Turn onto a floured board and shape into 2 balls. Let rest for 10 minutes. Roll each ball into 10 x 8-inch rectangle, then roll as for jelly roll, beginning at long end. Seal edges. Place rolls on greased baking sheet and slash tops diagonally 6 times. Cover with towel and let rise for 1 hour and 30 minutes. Bake at 400 degrees for 30 minutes.

Mrs. Carolyn James, Jackson, Mississippi

ALABAMA BISCUITS

1 pkg. yeast	2 tsp. baking powder
4 tsp. sugar	4 tbsp. shortening
2 1/2 c. flour	3/4 c. milk
1 tsp. salt	Melted butter

Dissolve the yeast with 1 teaspoon sugar in a small amount of warm water. Mix the dry ingredients and remaining sugar together in a mixing bowl, then cut in the shortening. Add the milk and yeast mixture. Roll out and cut with a small cutter. Dip each biscuit into butter and place on a baking sheet. Let rise for 1 hour. Bake at 450 degrees for 10 to 12 minutes.

Mrs. Rudolph F. Jones, Rocky Mount, Virginia

FRUIT WHIP

1 env. unflavored gelatin	Several drops of almond
1/4 c. fresh lime juice	extract
1 tsp. grated lime rind	1 c. chilled evaporated milk
3/4 c. fruit cocktail syrup	1 1/2 c. canned fruit cocktail,
1/2 c. sugar	drained
1/4 tsp. salt	Ladyfingers (opt.)

Soften the gelatin in the lime juice. Combine the lime rind, syrup, sugar, salt and gelatin in a saucepan and heat, stirring, until gelatin is dissolved. Blend in the almond extract, then chill until slightly thickened. Whip the evaporated milk in a chilled bowl until light and fluffy and fold in the gelatin mixture. Fold in the fruit cocktail and chill until partially set. Line serving dish with ladyfingers and spoon fruit mixture into dish. Chill for several hours or overnight. Garnish with additional fruit cocktail, if desired. 6-8 servings.

Fruit Whip (above)

BLACKBERRY JAM CAKE

2 c. sifted flour	3 eggs, beaten
1 tsp. baking powder	1 c. plumped raisins
1 tsp. soda	1 c. buttermilk
1 tsp. cinnamon	1 c. chopped pecans
2 c. sugar	1 pkg. flaked coconut
1 c. blackberry jam	

Sift the flour, baking powder, soda, cinnamon and sugar together in a bowl. Combine the remaining ingredients and mix, then add the flour mixture, mixing well. Turn into three 9-inch layer cake pans. Bake at 350 degrees for 30 to 40 minutes or until cake tests done.

Icing

4 tbsp. flour	1/4 c. blackberry jam
1 1/2 c. evaporated milk	1 c. ground raisins (opt.)
1 1/2 c. sugar	1 c. butter
1 c. flaked coconut	1 c. chopped nuts

Mix the flour to smooth paste with small amount of the milk, then combine all the ingredients in saucepan. Cook, stirring constantly, until of spreading consistency. Spread between layers and over side and top of cake.

Mrs. Emily Fischer, Corning, Arkansas

DELLA ROBIA COCONUT LAYER CAKE

1 c. shortening	3 c. sifted cake flour
2 c. sugar	2 1/4 tsp. baking powder
1/2 tsp. almond extract	3/4 tsp. salt
4 eggs	1 c. milk

Cream the shortening in a bowl. Add sugar gradually and beat until light and fluffy. Add the almond extract. Add the eggs, one at a time, beating well after each addition. Sift dry ingredients together and add to creamed mixture alternately with milk. Beat until smooth. Pour into 3 waxed paper-lined and greased 9-inch round layer pans. Bake at 375 degrees for about 25 minutes. Let stand for 5 minutes, then turn out on racks to cool.

Orange Filling

1/2 c. sifted cake flour	1/4 c. lemon juice
1 c. sugar	2 tbsp. grated orange rind
1/4 tsp. salt	Grated rind of 1 lemon
1/4 c. water	4 egg yolks, beaten slightly
1 1/4 c. orange juice	

Mix the flour, sugar and salt in a heavy saucepan. Add the water and mix until smooth. Add the orange juice, lemon juice, orange rind and lemon rind and mix. Cook over low heat until thickened and clear. Stir small amount into egg yolks and mix well. Stir back into sugar mixture and cook over low heat, stirring constantly, for about 5 minutes or until thick. Cool. Spread between cake layers.

Coconut Frosting

1 1/2 c. sugar	1/2 c. egg whites, stiffly
1/2 tsp. cream of tartar	beaten
1/8 tsp. salt	1/4 tsp. almond extract
1/2 c. hot water	2 c. grated coconut

Combine the sugar, cream of tartar, salt and hot water in a saucepan. Cook, without stirring, to 240 degrees on candy thermometer or to soft-ball stage. Add to egg whites slowly, beating constantly with rotary beater or electric mixer at high speed. Add the almond extract. Spread on top and side of cake and sprinkle with coconut.

Mrs. Joe Coats, Demopolis, Alabama

WATERMELON FRUIT BOWL

1 med. watermelon	Lemon juice
1 honeydew melon	2 c. red grapes
1 cantaloupe	2 c. green grapes
3 apples	1 c. dark sweet cherries

Cut watermelon in half lengthwise, then scoop out balls of melon with melon scoop and place in a large bowl. Scallop the edges of watermelon. Cut the honeydew and cantaloupe in half and scoop out balls. Mix all the melon balls together and chill. Core the apples and slice in thin wedges, then sprinkle with lemon juice. Combine all the fruits and place in watermelon shell. Garnish with mint sprigs.

Watermelon Fruit Bowl (above)

FRESH PEACH PIE

1 c. sugar	1 unbaked 9-in. pie shell
1/3 c. butter	Grated orange rind to taste
3/4 c. flour	6 med. peaches, diced

Mix the sugar, butter and flour together with a fork, then line the pie shell with half the sugar mixture. Sprinkle with orange rind. Place the peaches on the orange rind and add the remaining sugar mixture. Sprinkle with orange rind. Bake at 400 degrees for 15 minutes. Reduce oven temperature to 350 degrees and bake for 1 hour longer. Serve with whipped cream. 6-8 servings.

Mrs. Leah Fallon, Meridian, Mississippi

GRAND MARNIER CUSTARD

2 c. half and half	4 eggs
3 tbsp. Grand Marnier or other liqueur	4 egg yolks
	1/2 c. sugar

Combine the half and half with Grand Marnier in a saucepan and bring to boiling point. Cool slightly. Beat eggs and egg yolks with sugar in a bowl until light and lemon colored. Add the cream slowly and stir until blended. Strain through a fine sieve into a buttered baking dish and set the dish in a pan of hot water. Cover. Bake in a 350-degree oven for 35 to 45 minutes or until a knife inserted in the center comes out clean. Cool, then loosen from sides of dish with knife. Invert onto a serving plate. 4-6 servings.

Mrs. Mitchell Callis, Orlando, Florida

NEW ORLEANS PECAN PRALINES

1 1/2 c. pecan halves	1/3 stick butter
1 c. (packed) dark brown sugar	1/3 c. milk
1 c. sugar	1 tsp. vanilla

Combine the pecan halves, sugars and butter in a saucepan. Bring the milk to a boil and pour over the pecan mixture. Place over medium heat and cook for 7 minutes, stirring occasionally. Remove from heat and add the vanilla. Beat for about 30 seconds. Drop by tablespoonfuls onto waxed paper. 24 pralines.

Mrs. Marvin J. Lindsay, New Orleans, Louisiana

FESTIVE FIG PUDDING

2 lb. dried figs, chopped	3/4 c. sugar
1/2 lb. bread crumbs	1/4 c. milk
1/2 lb. ground suet	4 eggs, beaten

| 4 tsp. baking powder | 1/2 c. chopped nuts |
| 1/2 tsp. cinnamon | Hot lemon sauce |

Combine all ingredients except lemon sauce and mix well. Place in a greased mold and let stand for 1 hour. Place waxed paper or foil over mold and tie with string. Steam for 4 hours. Serve with lemon sauce.

Mrs. Andrew J. Snow, St. Petersburg Beach, Florida

SWEET POTATO-NUT PIE

Pastry for 1 9-in. pie	1/2 tsp. ginger
1/2 c. chopped pecans	1/2 tsp. salt
3 eggs, slightly beaten	1/4 c. lemon juice
1 c. (packed) brown sugar	2 tbsp. melted butter
1 c. milk	1 1/2 c. sieved cooked sweet
1 tsp. cinnamon	potatoes
1/2 tsp. nutmeg	1 1/2 c. whipped cream

Line a pie pan with the pastry, then press 1/4 cup of the pecans into the pastry. Combine the eggs, brown sugar, milk, cinnamon, nutmeg, ginger and salt in a bowl and mix well. Add the lemon juice and butter, beating until well blended. Blend in the sweet potatoes and remaining pecans, then pour into the pastry shell. Bake in 375-degree oven for about 50 minutes to 1 hour or until knife inserted near center of pie comes out clean. Top with the whipped cream. 8 servings.

Sweet Potato-Nut Pie (above)

favorite foods
of florida

Southerners are proud to count Florida as part of their region. Yet even they know that there are some things in this state that set it apart from the rest of the Deep South. It is not just that Florida is tropical; it is more that here the people have adapted to the land rather than expecting the land to conform to their wishes.

Perhaps nowhere else is this so well demonstrated as in the pages that follow. Side-by-side, you'll find recipes typical of the best of Deep South cooking, dishes with a faint hint of the Caribbean, and foods that could only be prepared in a region abounding with citrus fruits and readily available vegetables.

Suwannee River Catfish Chowder is a good example of the fine traditional recipes in this section. Obviously, some of the people who settled Florida from other parts of the Deep South brought their love of catfish with them! Other fish are prominently featured on Florida menus, even as they are throughout the region.

The recipe for Southern Ambrosia Parfait bridges the gap between the Deep South aspect of Florida and its uniqueness. This blend of coconut and citrus fruits is so traditional a dish that it is an inherent part of Christmas dinners from Maryland southward.

So, whether your pleasure is traditional southern cooking or foods unique to Florida, turn the pages of this section to find recipe after recipe that will hold your interest.

Florida is part of the Deep South and yet both its history and traditions reflect one important difference between it and the rest of the region. Settlers in other parts of the Deep South found land they could farm with familiar crops. The foods they grew and those they found in the rivers and woods could be adapted to familiar recipes. From Maryland to Louisiana during the first hundred and fifty years of the Deep South's history, intrepid settlers tamed nature and adjusted it to fit their lifestyle. They compromised sometimes, but what emerged was recognizable as having been influenced by the lifestyles of the Old World.

But not in Florida. This subtropical peninsula, jutting out between the Atlantic Ocean and the Gulf of Mexico, defied taming by anyone. Over

HISTORY AND TRADITIONS OF

of florida

many years of unsuccessful attempts at settling this wilderness land and transforming it into neat cotton and tobacco plantations similar to those in the rest of the Deep South, people came to realize that they, not the land, would have to change.

The first people to discover the riches of Florida were the Spaniards. Florida was only a short sail away from the center of their New World empire, Havana. The *adelantados,* the advancers, like Ponce de Leon, Fernando de Soto, and Panfilo de Narvaez explored the peninsula thoroughly during the middle and later parts of the 1500's. It is thanks to these explorers that oranges, lemons, and other citrus fruits were introduced into Florida. They planted the seeds, then were so busy exploring for gold that they let the crops grow wild. Although they never found gold, the Spanish did find wood, a precious enough crop for a nation that was concentrating on expanding its armada of wooden ships. Small, fortified Spanish settlements were established first at St. Augustine and Pensacola. From here lumber was shipped down the Gulf to Havana, and prepared there for trans-Atlantic shipment to Spain. During the 1600's the Spanish continued to establish only beachhead colonies in Florida and never did exploit the true richness of the land.

By the 1700's, the English colonies to the north of Florida were eyeing the region with envy. It was virtually unexplored by them, but they had heard of rich soil and plentiful trees. As the Carolinas and Georgia became increasingly crowded and land for plantations was scarce, more and more colonists began to edge down toward Florida.

The Spanish were caught in a double squeeze. Their hold on their New World empire was weakening, and they were unable to compete with thriving England and France. English colonies to the north threatened the Florida peninsula while a prosperous string of French settlements to the west threatened what is today the Florida panhandle. Finally, in 1763, Spain ceded Florida's peninsula to England. That was the signal that hundreds of would-be colonists needed to head south.

Among the first settlers were a group not of Englishmen or Americans but of Greeks, Italians, and Minorcans. They were recruited by a profit-minded Englishman to settle in Florida and grow indigo, then a rich source of income for many businessmen. They arrived in 1764 and settled the community of New Smyrna, about 60 miles south of St. Augustine. For a while they were content to combat the jungle-like land and raise indigo for their English master. Then their attention turned to the food-laden seas. They found that the waters off their settlement yielded shrimp and other seafood similar to that of their homeland. Moreover, the land would grow lemons, eggplant, and olives — all staples of their accustomed diet. Slowly the growing of indigo gave way to the establishment of a Mediteranean bastion and small farms emerged along the coast south of St. Petersburg. The Minorcans, as they were called, had found that by adapting themselves to the land they fared much better than they would have if they tried to force the land to adapt to them.

Similar discoveries were made by English and American settlers who tried to create cotton plantations inland. Here they found the freely-growing groves of citrus fruits left by the Spanish. It proved far easier to control the growth of what was already there than to force the land to grow cotton, and so small citrus farms began to emerge.

Even the return of Florida to Spain in 1783 did not discourage these small settlements. No cities comparable to Charleston or New Orleans were developed, but none seemed necessary in a land where so much pleasure could be derived simply from being outdoors.

Yet for all its differences from the rest of the Deep South, Florida has always been essentially southern. Those courageous families who first settled the region were for the most part from Georgia, Alabama, and the Carolinas. They brought with them their own cuisine, one that by the late 1700's was fairly well developed. This cuisine was altered by the introduction of salads and substantial quantities of citrus fruits to replace the heavy starches so prominent in other parts of the region. But ham, chicken, and greens remained important staple foods of the Florida settlers as they were in homes throughout the Deep South. Even the houses these newcomers built echo those found from Maryland's Chesapeake Bay to the river settlements of Alabama, Mississippi, and Louisiana.

Even the events of the years following 1821, when Florida finally became part of the United States, could not alter its southern-ness. Neither the introduction of railroad systems, tourists, nor massive beachfront hotels could alter the fact that Florida in its history, traditions, and cuisine is a very special part of the Deep South.

FLORIDA CONCH CHOWDER

2 1/2 lb. cooked conch meat	1 lge. potato, cut into
1/2 lb. sliced bacon,	cubes
chopped	1 tbsp. long grain rice
2 med. onions, sliced	3 bay leaves
1 1/2 tsp. minced garlic	1 qt. water
4 med. ripe tomatoes,	1 lge. can evaporated milk
chopped	

Grind the conch meat fine and place in a small bowl. Fry the bacon in a heavy 6-quart saucepan over moderate heat, stirring frequently, until crisp. Add the onions and garlic and cook, stirring frequently, for about 5 minutes or until the onions are soft but not brown. Stir in the conch meat, tomatoes, potato, rice, bay leaves and water and bring to a boil. Reduce heat and simmer, partially covered, for 1 hour, stirring frequently. Pour in the evaporated milk and cook, stirring, until heated through. Serve at once. Do not substitute fresh milk for evaporated milk. 6-8 servings.

Mrs. Ethelene Quigley, Tampa, Florida

SHRIMP STEW

1/2 c. flour	2 c. water
4 tbsp. bacon grease	2 c. cleaned fresh shrimp
1/2 c. chopped onions	1/2 tsp. salt
1/4 c. chopped green pepper	Hot sauce to taste (opt.)

Brown the flour in bacon grease in a saucepan until dark brown but not burned, stirring constantly. Add the onions and green pepper and cook, stirring, until onions are tender. Add the water, shrimp, salt and hot sauce and simmer for 20 to 30 minutes. Serve over rice. 4 servings.

Mrs. Louis F. Crawford, Long Beach, Mississippi

SUWANNEE RIVER CATFISH CHOWDER

20 lb. large catfish	10 bay leaves, crumbled
20 lb. potatoes, cubed	2 tbsp. thyme
4 1-lb. cans tomatoes	4 tbsp. seafood seasoning
2 8-oz. cans tomato sauce	1/2 c. Worcestershire sauce
10 lb. onions, chopped	Salt and pepper to taste
1 lb. butter or margarine	

Place the catfish in a kettle and cover with water. Bring to a boil. Reduce heat and simmer until catfish is well done. Strain the catfish and pour the liquid back into the kettle. Remove catfish from bones and place in the kettle. Add the potatoes and remaining ingredients and simmer for 2 hours, stirring frequently. Serve with saltines and pickles. 40 servings.

Herman Hooper, Mayo, Florida

APALACHICOLA CRAB SALAD

1 lb. white lump crab meat
1 lge. onion, cut into rings
1 c. salad oil
1/2 c. wine vinegar

1/2 c. water
Salt and pepper to taste
1 clove of garlic

Remove shell bits and cartilage from crab meat and place the crab meat in a bowl. Add the onion rings and toss well. Mix the oil, vinegar, water, salt and pepper. Pierce the garlic with a toothpick and add to the oil mixture. Pour over the crab meat mixture and cover tightly. Refrigerate for several hours, shaking well several times. Remove the garlic and drain the crab meat and onions. Serve on lettuce. May be topped with mayonnaise, if desired. 4 servings.

Mrs. Sarrah Glover, Quincy, Florida

TOMATO ASPIC

1 pkg. lemon gelatin
1 pkg. orange gelatin
2 8-oz. cans tomato sauce
3 tbsp. vinegar

1 tsp. celery salt
1 tsp. onion juice
1/2 tsp. sugar

Dissolve the gelatins in 2 cups hot water, then add the remaining ingredients. Pour into lightly oiled fluted mold and chill until firm. Unmold onto serving plate and garnish with lettuce. Serve with sour cream dressing. Yield: 6-8 servings.

Tomato Aspic (above)

FLORIDA FRUIT SALAD

1 mango	1 avocado
1 orange	1 c. grated coconut
1 pineapple	1/2 c. maraschino cherries (opt.)
1 papaya	Mayonnaise

Peel and cube the mango, orange, pineapple, papaya and avocado and mix. Add the coconut, cherries and enough mayonnaise to moisten and mix well. 6-8 servings.

Mrs. Bessie E. Briley, Ft. Lauderdale, Florida

HEARTS OF PALM SALAD

1 can hearts of palm, drained	Homemade mayonnaise or sour cream
Lettuce leaves	1 sm. jar black caviar

Chill all ingredients. Slice the hearts of palm lengthwise and arrange on lettuce leaves on individual salad plates. Spoon the mayonnaise over hearts of palm and add the caviar. 4-6 servings.

Mrs. Fred Berger, Hobe Sound, Florida

SOUTHERN ROAST BEEF

1 3 1/2-lb. eye of bottom beef round	2 tbsp. wine vinegar
1/4 c. soy sauce	Salt and pepper to taste
1 c. orange or pineapple juice	Flour

Place the beef in oblong baking pan. Combine the soy sauce, orange juice and vinegar and pour over beef. Cover and refrigerate overnight, turning beef several times. Drain and reserve marinade. Sprinkle beef with salt and pepper. Roast in 375-degree oven for 30 to 40 minutes or until brown. Add reserved marinade and cover. Roast for 2 hours and 30 minutes to 3 hours or until beef is tender. Remove beef to a platter, then cool and slice. Thicken the marinade sauce with flour mixed with water and add the slices of beef.

Mrs. Philip J. Mallon, Boca Raton, Florida

ELEGANT STEAK WITH OYSTERS

1 sirloin steak, 1 1/2 in. thick	4 tbsp. flour
Marjoram to taste	1/4 c. dry white wine
Thyme and savory to taste	2 c. chicken broth
Butter	2 egg yolks, beaten
Garlic salt to taste	1 qt. select oysters, drained

Slash the steak fat in several places and sprinkle one side of steak with the marjoram, thyme and savory. Let stand for 30 minutes. Place in a broiler pan, herb side up, and dot with butter. Broil to desired doneness. Turn and sprinkle with garlic salt. Dot with butter. Broil to desired doneness. Place on a heated platter and pour pan drippings over steak. Melt 4 tablespoons butter in a saucepan and stir in the flour. Stir in the wine and broth and bring to a boil, stirring constantly. Stir small amount of broth mixture into the egg yolks, then stir back into the broth mixture. Keep hot, but do not boil. Saute the oysters in small amount of butter until edges curl. Add oysters to sauce. Place the oysters on the platter around the steak and spoon small amount of sauce over the oysters. Serve remaining sauce with steak.

Mrs. Jesse Johnson, New Smyrna Beach, Florida

BUTTERMILK MEAT LOAF RING

2 tbsp. butter	1/8 tsp. pepper
1/3 c. chopped onions	1 1/2 lb. ground chuck
1 egg, slightly beaten	2 tbsp. chopped parsley
3/4 c. buttermilk	1/4 c. catsup
1/3 c. quick-cooking oatmeal	1 recipe mashed potatoes
1/2 tsp. monosodium glutamate	1/2 c. shredded cheese
1 tsp. salt	

Preheat oven to 350 degrees. Melt the butter in a small skillet, then add the onions and saute until tender. Combine the egg, buttermilk, oatmeal, monosodium glutamate, salt and pepper in a mixing bowl and mix thoroughly. Add the ground chuck, parsley and onions and blend thoroughly. Pack firmly into a ring mold. Bake for 1 hour and 15 minutes. Remove from oven and allow to stand for 5 minutes. Drain off excess drippings and turn out onto an ovenproof platter. Drizzle catsup over top of meat loaf and fill center with potatoes. Sprinkle the potatoes with the cheese and return to the oven. Bake until the cheese is melted.

Buttermilk Meat Loaf Ring (above)

DEER STEAK

1 round deer steak, 3/4 in. thick	Salt and pepper to taste
1/2 c. buttermilk	1/4 tsp. celery salt
1/2 c. flour	1/2 tsp. onion salt

Cut the steak into 4 pieces and pound with a meat hammer until tender. Dip in buttermilk, then dredge with flour. Brown on both sides in small amount of bacon drippings in a skillet, then sprinkle with seasonings. Bake at 350 degrees for 30 minutes. Mushroom soup may be poured over steak before baking, if desired.

Mrs. Alfred Peace, Mount Home, Arkansas

SMOTHERED RABBIT

1 rabbit	1 lge. onion, chopped
1 bay leaf, crumbled	1 sm. green pepper, chopped
Grated rind of 1 orange	1 stalk celery, chopped
2 c. wine	1 lge. can tomatoes
1 clove of garlic, minced	

Cut the rabbit into serving pieces and place in a bowl. Mix the bay leaf, grated rind and wine and pour over the rabbit. Refrigerate overnight. Drain the rabbit and wash thoroughly. Fry in small amount of fat in a deep skillet until brown. Add remaining ingredients except tomatoes and cook until the rabbit is nearly done. Add the tomatoes and cook until rabbit is done, adding water, if needed. Serve with rice. 4 servings.

Mrs. Fanny K. Vidos, Morgan City, Louisiana

BARBECUED SPARERIBS

3 lb. lean spareribs	1 tbsp. Worcestershire sauce
1 onion, finely chopped	2 tsp. chili powder
1 c. catsup	1 tsp. salt
2 c. water	1 tsp. pepper
1/4 c. vinegar	

Cut the spareribs into serving pieces and place in a baking pan. Combine remaining ingredients and pour over the spareribs. Cover. Bake at 350 degrees until meat of spareribs is tender, turning once. 6 servings.

Mrs. Frank Mayo, Eustis, Florida

HAM-BROCCOLI STRATA

12 slices bread	2 c. diced cooked ham
3/4 lb. sliced sharp American cheese	3 1/2 c. milk
1 10-oz. package frozen chopped broccoli, thawed	2 tbsp. instant minced onion
	1/2 tsp. salt
	1/4 tsp. dry mustard

Cut doughnut shapes from bread and set doughnuts and holes aside. Tear remaining bread in pieces and place in bottom of 13 x 9 x 2-inch baking dish. Place the cheese over bread and add broccoli. Add the ham. Arrange bread doughnuts on top and place holes between doughnuts. Combine remaining ingredients and pour over bread. Cover and refrigerate for at least 6 hours or overnight. Bake at 325 degrees for 55 minutes. Let stand for 10 minutes, then cut into squares. 12 servings.

Mrs. C. J. Cates, Birmingham, Alabama

PORK ROLLS WITH FENNEL

2 yellow onions	Salt and pepper to taste
3 tomatoes	Grated rind of 1 lge. orange
1 stand fennel	1 1/2 tsp. crushed rosemary
Margarine	2 c. beef stock
8 slices pork shoulder	1 tbsp. soy sauce

Slice the onions and tomatoes. Cut the fennel in half lengthwise and slice thinly. Place the onions, tomatoes and fennel in a skillet with a small amount of margarine and saute lightly, stirring frequently. Sprinkle the pork with the salt, pepper, orange rind and rosemary, then roll up and secure with picks. Brown the rolls on all sides in a small amount of fat in a frypan. Remove the rolls from frypan and place on vegetables in skillet. Add the beef stock and soy sauce. Simmer for 30 minutes. Garnish with parsley, if desired.

Pork Rolls with Fennel (above)

Boar's Head Turkey (below)

BOAR'S HEAD TURKEY

1 12-lb. turkey	1 tbsp. chopped parsley
Filbert Stuffing	1/4 tsp. marjoram
1 1/2 c. claret	1/4 tsp. thyme
1/2 c. melted butter	1/2 c. sifted flour
1 tbsp. lemon juice	Salt to taste
1 tbsp. chopped fresh chives	Freshly ground pepper to taste

Stuff body and neck cavities of the turkey with the Filbert Stuffing, then secure openings with skewers. Place in a roasting pan. Combine the claret, butter, lemon juice, chives, parsley, marjoram and thyme, then baste the turkey. Bake at 325 degrees for 25 minutes per pound, basting frequently with the sauce. Strain 1/2 cup of the pan drippings into a saucepan, then stir in flour. Stir in 2 cups water gradually, then cook, stirring, until gravy boils 1 minute. Season with salt and pepper. Place any remaining stuffing in a baking dish and cover tightly. Bake with turkey for 1 hour and 30 minutes. Place the turkey on a platter.

Filbert Stuffing

3/4 c. chopped onions	3/4 c. chopped parsley
1 c. butter	1/4 c. chopped celery
4 qt. cubed bread	1 cooked turkey liver, chopped
2 c. toasted chopped filberts	1/2 c. milk

Saute the onions in the butter in a skillet until crisp tender. Add to the remaining ingredients and mix well.

Vegetable Garland

3 15-oz. cans whole baby carrots	1 1/2 lb. mushrooms Butter
5 lb. new potatoes, pared	3 c. whole toasted filberts
3 10-oz. packages frozen California Brussels sprouts	2 tsp. lemon juice 6 tbsp. chopped chives
2 1/2 lb. pearl onions, peeled	6 tbsp. chopped parsley
6 ears of corn, halved	1 tsp. tarragon leaves

Place the carrots with liquid in a baking dish, then cover. Bake at 325 degrees for 40 minutes. Place the potatoes, Brussels sprouts, onions and corn in boiling salted water in separate saucepans. Cook until tender, then drain. Saute the mushrooms in 1/4 cup butter until golden brown. Arrange the vegetables and filberts on platter around the turkey. Melt 1 1/2 cups butter in a saucepan, then add the remaining ingredients and heat through. Serve the butter mixture with the vegetables.

CARIBBEAN CHICKEN

1 2-lb. fryer, quartered	1/2 c. water
1 1/4 c. olive oil	2 tsp. angostura bitters
4 sm. onions	6 lge. yams, cooked
3 tomatoes, quartered	3 tbsp. butter
4 med. carrots, halved	1/2 c. molasses

Brown the chicken in olive oil in a skillet, then place in a Dutch oven. Brown the onions, tomatoes and carrots in remaining oil in the skillet, then add to chicken. Add the water and 1 teaspoon angostura bitters and cover. Cook over low heat for 30 minutes or until chicken is tender. Peel and halve the yams. Melt the butter in a skillet and add the molasses and remaining angostura bitters. Add yams and cook, turning frequently, until glazed and heated through. Place the yams on a platter and place chicken and vegetables on the yams. Garnish with parsley. 4 servings.

Mrs. E. A. Getman, Bradenton, Florida

SPANISH-FRIED CHICKEN

1 frying chicken, disjointed	4 tbsp. butter
1 med. onion, chopped	2 tomatoes, chopped
1 bell pepper, chopped	2 1/2 c. water
1 c. rice	Salt to taste
1/2 tbsp. chili powder	

Brown the chicken and onion in butter, then place in a casserole. Mix remaining ingredients and place over chicken. Cover. Bake at 350 degrees for 40 minutes or until chicken is tender and rice is done. 4 servings.

Edna McSpadden, Bradford, Arkansas

CASSEROLE OF CHICKEN

1 chicken and giblets	2 med. onions, sliced
2 c. water	1 c. green peas
1 tsp. salt	1 c. sliced mushrooms
1 c. seasoned flour	1 1/2 c. sliced tomatoes
1/2 c. margarine	

Chop the giblets and place in a saucepan with water and salt. Cook for 45 minutes. Cut the chicken in serving pieces and roll in seasoned flour. Brown in margarine in a skillet and place in casserole. Saute onions in skillet drippings until tender and place over chicken. Stir remaining seasoned flour into skillet drippings. Add giblets and liquid gradually and cook, stirring, until thickened. Pour over chicken mixture and cover. Bake at 325 degrees for 1 hour and 30 minutes. Add the peas, mushrooms and tomatoes and bake for 15 minutes longer. 6-8 servings.

Mrs. John Adkins, Miami, Florida

COUNTRY-FRIED CATFISH

3 eggs, beaten	2 c. flour
1/4 c. milk	2 c. dry bread crumbs
1 1/2 tsp. salt	25 6-oz. pan-dressed catfish
1/4 tsp. pepper	

Combine the eggs, milk, salt and pepper and mix. Combine the flour and bread crumbs. Dip the catfish in the egg mixture, then roll in the flour mixture. Fry in deep fat at 350 degrees until brown and flakes easily when tested with a fork. Drain on absorbent paper. Arrange on tray and garnish with apple rings and lemon slices. Serve with hush puppies and tartar sauce.

Country-Fried Catfish (above)
Hush Puppies (page 183)

BROILED FISH STEAKS WITH CAPER SAUCE

1 tsp. lemon juice	6 fish steaks, 1 in. thick
1/4 c. sherry	1 tsp. salt
4 tbsp. capers	1/4 tsp. pepper
1 recipe white sauce	1/2 tsp. tarragon
6 tbsp. cooking oil	

Add the lemon juice, sherry and capers to the white sauce and mix well. Brush the oil over the fish steaks and season with salt, pepper and tarragon. Place steaks in a broiler pan and broil for 5 minutes. Turn and broil for 3 minutes longer. Place on a heated platter and garnish with lemon wedges and parsley sprigs. Serve with the caper sauce. Fish steaks may be cooked over hot coals, if desired.

Mrs. Gordon C. Bowen, Crystal River, Florida

BROILED POMPANO PENSACOLA

1 1 1/2-lb. pompano	1 tbsp. Worcestershire sauce
Salt and pepper to taste	3 tbsp. lemon juice
4 tbsp. melted butter	

Season the pompano with salt and pepper. Line a shallow baking pan with foil and place the pompano, dark side down, on foil. Mix the butter, Worcestershire sauce and lemon juice. Broil the pompano about 5 inches from heat for 8 minutes, basting frequently with lemon mixture. Turn and broil for 8 minutes longer or until fish flakes easily when tested with a fork, basting frequently with lemon mixture. Larger pompano may be split before broiling, if desired. 2 servings.

Mrs. Andrew C. Hinton, Pensacola, Florida

FISH WITH SHRIMP SAUCE

1 4 1/2-oz. can shrimp	1/8 tsp. cayenne pepper
3 tbsp. butter	1/4 tsp. dry mustard
1 4-oz. can mushrooms, drained	1/2 tsp. monosodium glutamate
1/4 c. flour	1 egg yolk, slightly beaten
1 1/2 c. milk	2 tsp. lemon juice
1 tsp. salt	6 fish fillets
1/8 tsp. white pepper	

Drain and rinse the shrimp. Melt the butter in a saucepan. Add the mushrooms and saute for several minutes. Blend in the flour. Add the milk and seasonings and cook over medium heat, stirring constantly, until thickened. Stir small amount of sauce into egg yolk, then stir back into the sauce. Cook and stir until thick. Remove from heat and stir in juice and shrimp. Place each fillet in a small, greased brown paper bag and spoon the shrimp mixture over each fillet. Fold bag ends under. Place in a baking pan. Bake at 400 degrees for 25 minutes.

Katie Lou Culpepper, Milton, Florida

BAKED FLORIDA RED SNAPPER WITH STUFFING

1 3 to 4-lb. dressed red snapper 1 1/2 tsp. salt	Sour Cream Stuffing Salad oil

Sprinkle the snapper inside and out with salt. Stuff with the Sour Cream Stuffing and secure opening with small skewers or toothpicks. Place in a well-greased baking pan and brush with oil. Bake in 350-degree oven for 45 to 60 minutes or until fish flakes easily when tested with a fork, brushing occasionally with oil. Remove skewers.

Sour Cream Stuffing

3/4 c. chopped celery	1/2 c. sour cream
1/2 c. chopped onion	1/4 c. diced lemon
1/4 c. oil	2 tbsp. paprika
4 c. dry bread cubes	1 tsp. salt

Cook the celery and onion in oil until tender. Add remaining ingredients and mix thoroughly.

Mrs. Peter A. Lutz, Cocoa Beach, Florida

CRAB DIABLE

6 tbsp. butter or margarine	1/8 tsp. white pepper
1/2 tsp. marjoram	1/2 c. light cream
2/3 c. crushed bite-size shredded wheat cereal	1 tbsp. Worcestershire sauce
1 tbsp. flour	2 eggs, well beaten
1 tsp. dry mustard	2 c. flaked crab meat
1/2 tsp. salt	1/2 c. minced celery

Melt 1 tablespoon butter in a saucepan over low heat and stir in the marjoram. Stir in the cereal crumbs until coated with butter mixture. Melt remaining butter in top of a double boiler over boiling water and stir in flour, mustard, salt and pepper. Blend in the cream, Worcestershire sauce and eggs and stir for 15 minutes or until thick. Add the crab meat and celery. Spoon into individual baking shells and top with buttered cereal crumbs. Place in a baking pan. Bake at 325 degrees for 20 minutes. 4-6 servings.

Mrs. Harry E. Stalker, Bradenton, Florida

FLORIDA LOBSTER AU GRATIN

4 tbsp. butter	1 tsp. Worcestershire sauce
4 tbsp. flour	1 tbsp. lemon juice
1 tsp. salt	2 c. cooked lobster meat
1/8 tsp. pepper	1 c. soft bread crumbs
1 3/4 c. milk	2 tbsp. melted butter
1/2 c. thin cream	

Melt the butter in a saucepan and stir in flour, salt and pepper. Add the milk and cream slowly and cook over low heat, stirring constantly, until mixture thickens and boils. Stir in the Worcestershire sauce, lemon juice and lobster meat and place in a greased 1 1/2-quart baking dish. Mix the crumbs and melted butter and sprinkle over lobster mixture. Bake at 425 degrees for 15 minutes or until golden brown. 6 servings.

Mrs. Charles E. Rolph, Homestead, Florida

TOP HAT RAISIN-LOBSTER CURRY

1/2 c. California seedless raisins	1/2 c. chicken broth
1/2 tsp. curry powder	1 egg yolk, lightly beaten
1/4 tsp. paprika	1/2 c. half and half
2 tbsp. butter	1 tbsp. sherry
1 tbsp. flour	1 tbsp. chopped pimento
1/2 tsp. seasoned salt	1 1/2 c. cubed cooked lobster
	4 patty shells

Cook the raisins, curry powder and paprika in the butter in a saucepan for several minutes. Blend in the flour and salt, then stir in the broth slowly. Cook, stirring, until thickened. Mix the egg yolk with the half and half and stir into the sauce. Cook for several minutes longer. Blend in the sherry, pimento and lobster and spoon into patty shells. Serve with accompaniments of California dark and golden seedless raisins, shredded coconut, sliced green onions and crumbled crisp bacon. 4 servings.

Top Hat Raisin-Lobster Curry (above)

QUAIL AND OYSTERS

Quail	Butter
Oysters	Salt and pepper to taste
Melted butter	Sliced bacon
Cornmeal	Sherry to taste
Flour	Cooked wild rice

Wipe the quail inside and out with a damp cloth. Dip the oysters in melted butter, then dip in cornmeal. Place 3 oysters inside each quail. Mix enough flour and butter to make a paste and rub on quail. Season with salt and pepper. Place the quail in a baking dish and place 1 strip bacon across each quail. Add sherry. Bake at 350 degrees for 30 minutes, basting with melted butter occasionally. Serve on wild rice.

Mrs. William B. Nunn, Tallahassee, Florida

OYSTERS BORDELAISE

3 doz. oysters on half shells	2 tbsp. minced shallots or scallions
Rock salt	1/2 c. dry red wine
1 tsp. salt	Bread crumbs
1/2 tsp. paprika	

Place the oysters on a layer of rock salt in a baking pan. Mix the salt, paprika, shallots and wine and spoon over the oysters. Sprinkle with bread crumbs. Bake at 425 degrees for 3 to 5 minutes or until the oysters are heated through. 6 servings.

Mrs. John Cicale, Milton, Florida

FLORIDIAN-STYLE CRAB

2 med. avocados	1 can cream of mushroom soup
1/2 lb. crab meat	2 tbsp. melted butter
3 tbsp. lemon juice	1 c. soft bread crumbs
1/2 tsp. salt	
1/2 tsp. pepper	

Peel and slice the avocados. Arrange alternate layers of avocados and crab meat in a greased 2-quart casserole, sprinkling each layer with lemon juice, salt and pepper. Cover with undiluted soup. Combine the butter and crumbs and sprinkle over top. Bake at 350 degrees for 20 minutes. Do not overcook. 4 servings.

Mrs. G. F. Drinkard, Tallahassee, Florida

ONION PIE

1 c. thinly sliced onions	1 unbaked 9-in. pie shell
2 tbsp. butter	3 eggs, slightly beaten

1 1/2 tbsp. flour
2 tsp. dry mustard

1/2 c. mayonnaise
1/2 c. evaporated milk

Saute the onions in butter until tender, then place in the pie shell. Blend the eggs and flour in a bowl and stir in the mustard, mayonnaise and evaporated milk. Pour over the onions. Bake at 350 degrees for 45 to 60 minutes or until firm. Let stand for 10 minutes before slicing.

Mrs. William N. Hooks, Ashdown, Arkansas

CORN ON THE COB

1 1/2 tsp. aniseed
1 stick butter

1 tsp. salt
8 ears of corn

Pour 1 1/2 teaspoons boiling water over the aniseed in a bowl and let stand for 30 minutes. Cream the butter until light and fluffy, then stir in the aniseed and salt. Cook the corn in enough boiling water to cover for 12 to 15 minutes or until tender. Serve with the butter mixture.

Mrs. H. H. Duncan, Knoxville, Tennessee

SOUTHERN-STYLE FRESH POLE BEANS

1/4 lb. salt pork
1 lb. pole beans

3/4 (about) tsp. salt
Onion rings

Wash the salt pork. Make a crosswise cut through the center down to the rind and then make 3 or 4 crosswise slashes. Place in a kettle with 1/2 inch boiling water. Cover and cook for 35 minutes or until the salt pork is tender. Remove tips from pole beans and cut into 1-inch pieces. Wash, then add to the pork along with the salt. Cover and cook for 20 minutes or until the beans are crisp-tender. Garnish with onion rings.6 servings.

Southern-Style Fresh Pole Beans (above)

CORN PUDDING

4 ears of corn	1 tsp. salt
4 eggs	1 tsp. sugar
2 c. milk	2 tbsp. bacon fat

Cut the corn from cobs and place in a blender container. Add remaining ingredients and blend well. Pour into a greased 1 1/2-quart casserole and place in a pan of water. Bake at 400 degrees for 45 minutes to 1 hour or until firm. 6 servings.

Mrs. J. A. Eshelman, High Point, North Carolina

AMERICAN-FRIED POTATOES

6 med. potatoes	1 tsp. salt
1/2 c. thinly sliced onions	1/8 tsp. pepper
1/4 c. shortening	

Slice or cube the potatoes and add onions. Heat the shortening in a 9-inch frying pan. Add potato mixture and fry over medium heat until golden brown, turning frequently. Season with salt and pepper. 4 servings.

Beulah McGlone, Olive Hill, Kentucky

SWEET POTATO PONE

2 1/2 c. grated sweet potatoes	2 tbsp. melted butter
1 c. sugar	1 c. chopped nuts
2 eggs, well beaten	1/4 tsp. cinnamon
1 tbsp. grated orange rind	3/4 c. milk
1 tsp. nutmeg	

Mix all ingredients and place in a greased casserole. Dot with additional butter. Bake at 350 degrees for about 45 minutes or until golden brown. 6 servings.

Mrs. Ruth Reams, Greenville, Florida

CORNMEAL CRESCENTS

3 tbsp. sugar	1/4 c. warm water
3/4 tbsp. salt	3/4 c. grated cheese
6 tbsp. shortening	2 eggs
3/4 c. milk, scalded	2 1/2 c. flour
1 pkg. yeast	3/4 c. cornmeal

Mix the sugar, salt, shortening and milk in a bowl and cool to lukewarm. Dissolve the yeast in water and add to milk mixture. Stir in the cheese and eggs.

Add the flour and cornmeal and mix until smooth. Refrigerate until chilled. Divide in half. Roll out each half on a floured surface to a circle and spread with additional butter. Cut into wedges and roll each wedge from wide end to point. Place on a greased baking sheet, point side down. Let rise until doubled in bulk. Bake at 375 degrees for 15 minutes.

Mrs. Dorothy Jean Worsham, Stilwell, Oklahoma

CORN WAFFLES

2 c. sifted flour	1 1/4 c. milk
3 tbsp. sugar	1 No. 303 can cream-style corn
3 tbsp. baking powder	1/2 c. melted butter or
1 tsp. salt	margarine
2 eggs, separated	

Sift the dry ingredients together into a bowl. Beat the egg yolks in a bowl until light, then add milk, corn and butter. Add to dry ingredients and mix well. Beat the egg whites until stiff but not dry and fold into batter. Bake in hot waffle iron until golden brown. 4 large waffles.

Mrs. W. A. Sheffield, New Castle, Delaware

HUSH PUPPIES

2 c. cornmeal	1 c. milk
1/2 c. flour	2 well-beaten eggs
1 tsp. baking powder	1 lge. onion, chopped
1 tsp. salt	1 tbsp. melted lard

Mix first 4 ingredients in a bowl. Add the milk, eggs and onion and mix well. Stir in the lard. Drop by spoonfuls into hot, deep fat and cook until brown. 6-8 servings.

Photograph for this recipe on page 176.

SOUR MILK BISCUITS

3 c. flour	1/2 c. shortening
4 tsp. baking powder	1 1/2 c. sour milk or
Pinch of soda	buttermilk
1 tsp. salt	Melted butter

Sift the dry ingredients together into a bowl and cut in shortening. Stir in the sour milk. Turn out onto a floured board and knead well. Roll out 1/2 inch thick and cut with a biscuit cutter. Place on a well-greased baking sheet and brush with butter. Bake in 450-degree oven until golden brown. 2 dozen.

Mrs. H. O. Boeneman, Houston, Texas

CITRUS CREAM PIE

1 3/8 c. sugar
3 tbsp. cornstarch
1/3 c. lemon or lime juice
1 1/2 c. orange juice

3 eggs, separated
2 tbsp. butter or margarine
1 baked pie shell

Combine 1 cup sugar, cornstarch, lemon juice and orange juice in saucepan and cook over medium heat until thick, stirring constantly. Stir small amount of cooked mixture into beaten egg yolks, then stir back into cooked mixture. Add butter and cook for 5 minutes longer. Pour into pie shell. Beat egg whites until stiff, adding remaining sugar gradually, and spread over filling. Bake at 425 degrees until brown.

Mrs. Henry Mayberry, Orlando, Florida

BANANA PUDDING

2 c. milk
2 eggs, beaten
2/3 c. sugar
1/8 tsp. salt

2 tbsp. cornstarch
1 tsp. vanilla
48 (about) vanilla wafers
4 bananas, diced

Combine first 5 ingredients in top of a double boiler and beat with an electric mixer until smooth. Place over hot water and cover. Cook, stirring occasionally, until thick, then cool. Stir in the vanilla. Place alternate layers of vanilla wafers, bananas and custard in a 1 1/2-quart casserole. Cover and chill, if desired. 6 servings.

Mrs. Ronald Rodgers, Dade City, Florida

COCONUT DELIGHT

2 2/3 c. cake flour
1 1/2 c. sugar
4 tsp. baking powder
1/4 tsp. salt

1/2 c. shortening
2 eggs
1 1/3 c. milk
2 tsp. vanilla

Sift the flour, sugar, baking powder and salt together into a bowl. Add the shortening, eggs and half the milk and beat for 1 minute with mixer at high speed. Mix remaining milk and vanilla and add to flour mixture gradually. Place in a greased 9 x 13-inch baking pan. Bake at 350 degrees for 30 minutes. Leave in pan.

Topping

1/2 stick butter
1 c. (packed) brown sugar
1/3 c. cream

1 can flaked coconut
1/2 c. chopped pecans

Mix the butter and sugar. Add the cream, coconut and pecans and mix well. Spread over cake carefully. Broil 6 to 8 inches from heat for 1 to 2 minutes or until bubbly, watching carefully.

Mrs. Lowell Hamilton, Panama City, Florida

FLORIDA ORANGE TORTE

1 18 1/2 or 19-oz. package yellow cake mix
1 6-oz. can frozen Florida orange juice concentrate, thawed

2 3 1/4-oz. packages vanilla pudding and pie filling
1/2 c. semisweet chocolate pieces
1 tbsp. light corn syrup

Prepare the cake mix according to package mixing directions and place in 2 greased and floured 8-inch square pans. Bake at 350 degrees for 25 to 30 minutes. Cool for 10 minutes, then remove from pan. Cool on racks. Reserve 2 tablespoons orange juice concentrate for glaze. Add enough water to the remaining concentrate to make 3 cups orange juice. Place the pudding in a saucepan. Add the orange juice and stir until blended. Cook over medium heat, stirring constantly, until mixture comes to a full boil. Place waxed paper directly on pudding and cool. Refrigerate for several hours. Remove the waxed paper and stir. Melt the chocolate pieces over hot, not boiling water, then remove from water. Stir in the corn syrup and reserved orange concentrate until smooth. Cut each cake layer in half horizontally. Place 1 layer on a serving plate and top with 1 cup pudding mixture. Repeat with the remaining cake layers and pudding mixture. Spread the chocolate mixture over top of the cake. Chill. 12-16 servings.

Florida Orange Torte (above)

MANGO PLEIN DE CREME

2 c. sliced mangos	**1 med. orange**
1 box dessert topping mix	**1/2 c. broken pecans (opt.)**

Puree mangos in blender. Prepare dessert topping mix according to package directions, reserving small amount for garnish. Peel the orange, remove seeds and cut orange in small pieces. Fold into dessert topping and fold in mangos and pecans. Spoon into sherbet or parfait glasses and garnish with reserved dessert topping. 6-9 servings.

Mrs. Edward H. Schmidt, Delray Beach, Florida

NECTARINE CHEESECAKE-PIE

2 or 3 fresh nectarines	**2 3-oz. packages cream**
1 unbaked 9-in. pastry shell	**cheese, softened**
3 eggs	**1 tsp. grated lemon rind**
1/2 c. whipping cream	**1 tsp. lemon juice**
1 1/4 c. powdered sugar	

Slice enough nectarines to make 1 2/3 cups and arrange in bottom of the pastry shell. Beat 2 eggs lightly with cream and 1 cup powdered sugar and pour over nectarines. Beat the cream cheese with lemon rind, lemon juice and remaining egg and sugar and spoon over the cream mixture. Bake in 375-degree oven for 30 minutes. Cool thoroughly. Cut 8 nectarine slices and arrange, petal-fashion, in center of pie. Blend additional cream cheese with milk until soft and dollop in center of pie, if desired. 6-8 servings.

Nectarine Cheesecake-Pie (above)

186

KEY LIME PIE

1 tbsp. unflavored gelatin	2 tbsp. angostura bitters
4 eggs, separated	Grated rind of 1 lime
1 c. sugar	1 baked pie crust
1/2 c. lime juice	1 c. heavy cream, whipped
1/2 tsp. salt	

Soften the gelatin in 1/2 cup water. Beat the egg yolks in top of a double boiler. Stir in 1/2 cup sugar, lime juice and salt and place over boiling water. Cook, stirring, until mixture coats the spoon. Remove from water. Add the gelatin, bitters and rind and mix well. Chill until thickened. Beat the egg whites in a bowl until stiff, adding remaining sugar gradually. Fold into the lime mixture and place in the pie crust. Chill until firm. Spread whipped cream over top.

Mrs. Foster Dulaney, Miami, Florida

FRESH COCONUT PIE

3 eggs	1 tsp. vanilla
1 1/2 c. sugar	1 fresh coconut, grated
2 tbsp. flour	1 1/2 c. milk
2 tbsp. melted butter	1 unbaked 9-in. pie shell

Beat the eggs slightly, then add the sugar, flour, butter, vanilla and coconut. Stir in the milk slowly, mixing well. Pour into the pie shell. Bake at 400 degrees until lightly browned and center is set.

Mrs. Llewellyn Spillman, Spillman, Louisiana

FRESH ORANGE DESSERT

Fresh sliced oranges	Fresh grated coconut
Boiled custard	

Place several orange slices in each dessert dish and cover with custard. Sprinkle with coconut.

Mrs. Mills E. Godwin, Jr., Richmond, Virginia

SOUTHERN AMBROSIA PARFAIT

1 c. milk	1 tsp. salt
1 c. heavy cream	3 tbsp. sherry
4 egg yolks	8 med. oranges, sectioned
1/4 c. sugar	1 1/2 c. grated coconut
1 tbsp. flour	

Pour the milk and cream into top of a double boiler and heat over boiling water until scalded. Beat egg yolks in a mixing bowl until light and stir in sugar, flour and salt. Add milk mixture slowly, stirring constantly. Return to double boiler and cook until thick. Cool, then add sherry. Place alternate layers of orange sections, custard and coconut in a serving dish, ending with coconut. Refrigerate until chilled.

Wynona H. White, Livingston, Alabama

ABBREVIATIONS, MEASURES, AND SUBSTITUTIONS

ABBREVIATIONS

Cup . . . . .c.		Large . . . . .lge.	
Tablespoon . . . . tbsp.		Package . . . . pkg.	
Teaspoon . . . . .tsp.		Small . . . . .sm.	
Pound . . . . lb.		Dozen . . . . doz.	
Ounce . . . . oz.		Pint . . . . pt.	

MEASURES

3 tsp. = 1 tbsp.	2 c. sugar = 1 lb.
2 tbsp. = 1/8 c.	5/8 c. = 1/2 c. + 2 tbsp.
4 tbsp. = 1/4 c.	7/8 c. = 3/4 c. + 2 tbsp.
8 tbsp. = 1/2 c.	2 2/3 c. powdered sugar = 1 lb.
16 tbsp. = 1 c.	2 2/3 c. brown sugar = 1 lb.
5 tbsp. + 1 tsp. = 1/3 c.	4 c. sifted flour = 1 lb.
12 tbsp. = 3/4 c.	1 lb. butter = 2 c. or 4 sticks
4 oz. = 1/2 c.	2 pt. = 1 qt.
8 oz. = 1 c.	1 qt. = 4 c.
16 oz. = 1 lb.	A few grains = less than 1/8 tsp.
1 oz. = 2 tbsp. fat or liquid	Pinch = as much as can be taken
2 c. fat = 1 lb.	between tip of finger and thumb
2 c. = 1 pt.	Speck = less than 1/8 tsp.

SUBSTITUTIONS

1 tablespoon cornstarch (for thickening) = 2 tablespoons flour (approximately)

1 cup sifted all-purpose flour = 1 cup plus 2 tablespoons sifted cake flour

1 cup sifted cake flour = 1 cup minus 2 tablespoons sifted all-purpose flour

1 teaspoon baking powder = 1/4 teaspoon baking soda plus 1/2 teaspoon cream of tartar

1 cup bottled milk = 1/2 cup evaporated milk plus 1/2 cup water

1 cup sour milk = 1 cup sweet milk into which 1 tablespoon vinegar or lemon juice has been stirred; or 1 cup buttermilk

1 cup sweet milk = 1 cup sour milk or buttermilk plus 1/2 teaspoon baking soda

1 cup cream, sour, heavy = 1/3 cup butter and 2/3 cup milk in any sour-milk recipe

1 cup cream, sour, thin = 3 tablespoons butter and 3/4 cup milk in sour-milk recipe

1 cup molasses = 1 cup honey

INDEX

PHOTOGRAPHY CREDITS: Reid Smith; U. S. Department of Commerce: National Marine Fisheries Service; Brussels Sprouts Marketing Program; National Cherry Growers and Industries Foundation; Standard Brands Products: Fleischmann's Yeast, Fleischmann's Margarine, Blue Bonnet Margarine; California Raisin Advisory Board; Quaker Oats Company; American Dairy Association; National Meat Canners Association; National Fisheries Institute; National Pecan Shellers and Processors Association; American Lamb Council; Spanish Green Olive Commission; Pickle Packers International; Louisiana Yam Commission; California Apricot Advisory Board; California Dried Fig Advisory Board; Filbert/Hazelnut Institute; Gerber Baby Foods; Pineapple Growers Association; International Shrimp Council; McCormick and Company, Inc.; National Dairy Council; The American Spice Trade Association; National Livestock and Meat Board; Cling Peach Advisory Board; Keith Thomas Company; North American Blueberry Council; Evaporated Milk Association; McIlhenny Company; United Fresh Fruit and Vegetable Association; Florida Citrus Commission; Apple Pantry: Washington State Apple Commission; California Avocado Advisory Board.

Printed in the United States of America.